Face-to-Face With the
Real
Gospel

Face-to-Face With the
Real
Gospel

Dennis E. Priebe

Pacific Press Publishing Association
Boise, Idaho
Montemorelos, Nuevo Leon, Mexico
Oshawa, Ontario, Canada

Designed by Tim Larson
Cover art by Nery Cruz

Copyright © 1985 by
Pacific Press Publishing Association
Printed in United States of America
All Rights Reserved

Library of Congress Cataloging in Publication Data

Priebe, Dennis E., 1942—
  Face to face with the real gospel.

  1. Salvation—History of doctrines—20th century. 2. Jesus Christ—
History of doctrines—20th century. 3. Seventh-Day Adventists—Doc-
trines—History—20th century. I. Title.
BX6154.P73   1985   230'.6732   85-12462
ISBN 0-8163-0617-6

  86 87 88 89 • 6 5 4 3 2

Contents

Will the Real Gospel Please Stand Up?

The past few years have been a painful time for Seventh-day Adventists. Most of us were not around when the Pantheism crisis struck the church early in this century and many leading lights left the organization. Through the intervening years we have all seen pastors leave the ministry for various reasons—including an occasional pastor who felt that Seventh-day Adventist beliefs were not compatible with his own. But now we are seeing young, bright, conscientious pastors saying, "I can no longer preach Adventism and be true to my conscience and the Bible."

Some church members have felt they were hearing a different brand of Adventism proclaimed from their pulpits—one totally incompatible with the Adventist mission and message. What is going on in our beloved church? Ministers and laymen alike have become increasingly confused. Booming salvos have been fired from both sides, while those in the middle wonder how they can possibly make a decision about who is right, or whether they should just silently slip out the back door of Adventism. Are there any answers, or are we doomed to stumble along while our church continues to suffer?

I am convinced that a reason exists for the pain we are suffering today, but that a solution also exists to our theological dilemma. We have been told that our church must be judged by the gospel. I accept that challenge. The gospel lies at the heart of Christianity, and without the gospel there would be no point or purpose in Sabbath keeping. But what is the gospel? This is the critical question that has been pounding at the consciousness of pastors, teachers, and laymen.

I am going to propose that there are two versions of the gospel being proclaimed within Adventism. I am going to outline them from presuppositions to conclusions, with the hope that doing so will explain why some men and women are having a crisis of conscience with Seventh-day Adventist teaching. Of course, I will specify which gospel I believe to be in harmony with the Bible and Adventism. But perhaps the greatest good to come from what I am about to say will be the clarification of the opposing positions so that you will be better prepared, individually, to study the Bible and our modern inspired source—the writings of Ellen White—to determine which of the two systems of belief will be *your* gospel. For ultimately it must come to that—you must make a decision based on Bible study and prayer.

You see, in the past it has been relatively easy to identify the "offshoot" groups and stay within the mainstream of Adventism. Not many have followed the voices of the Shepherd's Rod or the Reformed Adventists. But now we have two gospels within the mainstream of Adventism, which makes the choice much more difficult. For the past thirty years this has been developing within Adventism, and I submit that the events of the late 70s and early 80s are the inevitable and natural result of seeds planted many years ago. What we once thought to be one track of truth stretching out before us has been seen only lately as two tracks, diverging more and more widely until we have found ourselves at this crisis point. At the heart of my proposal is the deep conviction that these two tracks are totally incompatible with each other, that compromise or harmony between them is logically impossible, and that one *must* make a choice between the two systems. Then let us look at these rival claimants to the title "gospel" with the hope that the real gospel will be able to stand up confidently.

Statement of the Problem

In a recent article entitled "Exodus from Adventism," a list appeared of 100 Seventh-day Adventist ministers and teachers who have left Adventism for reasons of conscience. In the article was this comment: "The denomination would give the appearance that it is frantically attempting to rid itself of the unwelcome doctrines of salvation by faith alone and the all-sufficiency of Scripture as the sole doctrinal norm."—Sharon Herbey, "Exodus from Adventism," *Evangelica*, February 1982, p. 23. Now those are broad charges. Is it possible to be more specific about just what is meant here?

In South Africa, Francis Campbell, a former union conference president, attempted to pinpoint the specific areas of controversy in these words: "The denomination has never been able to define clearly its position on the nature of Christ, perfection, original sin—areas which are vital to an understanding of righteousness by faith. As a result various streams of theology exist within the church, leaving our members in a state of confusion."—*Ibid.*

I believe that his insights are extremely accurate and get to the heart of the difficulties we are experiencing. For I agree that as a church we have never formally defined our beliefs in these three critical areas—sin, Christ, and perfection. And because of our unclarity and divergent views in these areas, we have been wandering in the theological desert of uncertainty and frustration for these past forty years. Further, because we have held contradictory views in these areas, we have been unable clearly to define our message and our mission.

The following lines were written by Aage Rendalen, a former Seventh-day Adventist editor in Norway.

In the 1950s Adventism began a remarkable house cleaning. A number of doctrines which had bothered theological purists for years were given a public funeral. With the rising level of biblical knowledge in the church, as well as increasing contact with evangelical theologians, many leading Adventists felt embarrassed about some of the doctrines that had survived the nineteenth century. Chief among these were the doctrines of the split atonement and the sinful nature of Christ. With the publication of the book *Questions on Doctrine* in 1957 both views were repudiated.

The work of clarification progressed up to the beginning of the 1970s . By then the traditional belief in a latter day perfection had come under attack and seemed to be on the way out. . . . In spite of frantic efforts by a few vocal defenders of Adventist tradition, the doctrines of the sinful nature of Christ and human perfectibility in this world were slowly sinking. The weight of biblical evidence had simply overcome what little buoyancy was left.

With the dawning of the eighties a new crisis of unsurpassed magnitude is now confronting the church. What is thought to be the very foundation of Adventism—our 'sanctuary theology'—is coming under close examination. At the same time the authority of Mrs. White as a crypto-canonical prophet is being re-evaluated.

With the evangelical courtship of the 1950s the Adventist leaders started something the extent of which they did not anticipate. The traditional Adventist landscape was being radically changed, and as a result a crisis of identity set in. Today, the very validity of the movement has become an open question of many. They feel that this is not the church they joined. The doctrinal superiority. . . which the evangelist had held out to them now appears to lie in shambles. Can this really be "the only true church"? they ask.—Aage Rendalen, "Adventism: Has the Medium Become the Message?" *Evangelica,* December 1980, p. 35.

As I read this article, I got the feeling that, from a quite different perspective, Rendalen was stating what I want to state, for he has pinpointed the issues at stake in the controversy and the historical development of these issues over the past thirty years. He has, in fact, hit the nail squarely. These are the issues that need to be defined if there is any hope that the real gospel will ever stand up. I would like to repeat one exceedingly important passage in his article: "With the evangelical courtship of the 1950's the Adventist leaders started something the extent of which they did not anticipate. The traditional Adventist landscape was being radically changed." How very, very true.

I have come to believe that the things we have seen in the late 70s and early 80s are but the inevitable harvest of the seeds planted during the 50s and 60s. These theological seeds have matured into a consistent and logical theological harvest. By this I mean that, given certain presuppositions, certain conclusions are necessary, even inevitable, and many thinking Adventists have seen the necessity of living out the implications of those conclusions. Moreover, these differing, conflicting presuppositions and conclusions are widely believed right now *within* the Seventh-day Adventist Church by a wide range of scholars, ministers, and laymen.

Thus it is not just a matter of beliefs outside Adventism versus those within. Both systems of theological belief are alive and growing in the Seventh-day Adventist Church today. Now let us look more specifically at the individual components of these systems of belief.

The Central Issue

The pivotal issue, it seems to me, which determines the direction of both systems of belief—foundation and premise of the whole controversy—is the question, What is sin? After all, the gospel is all about how we are saved from sin. It is sin which has caused us to be lost, and the gospel is the good news of how God redeems us from sin. Now most of us it would seem have assumed, for perhaps our entire lifetime, that we know what sin is, but as is typically true for most things that we assume without examining them carefully, our assumptions may simply be unproved suppositions that need careful rethinking. It is just at this point that Adventism has been challenged as having unclear and even erroneous definitions of sin which have led to erroneous positions in righteousness by faith.

The crucial question is, What is the nature of sin for which man is considered guilty, so guilty that he must die in the fires of hell unless he is rescued by the grace of God? We must be precise in defining the nature of this sin, so that we will know just what it is that the gospel rescues us from. Of what must we be forgiven? What must be healed for us to escape eternal death? When you visit a physician, he must first determine precisely (we hope) the nature of the problem afflicting you before he can prescribe a therapy or medicine which can heal you. Just so with sin. We must know wherein our guilt lies, so that we will be able to apply the gospel to the correct illness.

The Gospel as Defined in "New" or "Reformation" Theology

The Nature of Sin

In Geoffrey Paxton's challenging book, *The Shaking of Adventism,* he says that Seventh-day Adventists rejected righteousness by faith in 1888 because we rejected the historic doctrine of original sin. He identifies original sin as the foundational principle of Reformation theology.—Pages 98-114. Now original sin is simply the belief that we are guilty before God because of our birth as sons and daughters of Adam. We are guilty by nature, before any choice of good or evil enters the picture. Our condemnation comes from Adam; we are guilty because of our inherited depravity. "There is sin in the desire of sin." "Sin is declared to exist in the being prior to our own consciousness of it." "There is guilt in evil desires, even when resisted by the will."—Desmond Ford, "The Relationship Between the Incarnation and Righteousness by Faith," in *Documents From the Palmdale Conference on Righteousness by Faith,* p. 28.

According to this view, sin and guilt apply to nature, and the gospel must deal with the reality of guilt as a part of the nature of man which can never be removed until we are given new bodies at Christ's second coming, when mortality puts on immortality. In this view, weakness, imperfection, and tendencies are sin. It is an interesting and significant point that the Reformers built their doctrine of original sin on the premise of predestination, which teaches that God leaves some men to suffer and die in their sinful and guilty natures while He elects to send His saving grace to others through the gospel. These two doctrines fit together naturally. Thus, it is a bit strange that while predestination has been rejected by many Christians today, original sin is still seen as the foundation of correct gospel teaching.

The Nature of Christ

Now to the next step, proceeding from this premise: What kind of human being must Christ be, if He is going to be both human and sinless? Obviously this point of view emphasizes He must have a sinless nature, totally unlike the nature you and I inherit from birth. Sometimes this position is referred to as "the nature of Adam before the fall," or prelapsarian nature. Some statements made by those who hold this view will help to clarify the point: "For Christ to be the second or last Adam He . . .

must possess a sinless Human Nature." "To teach that Christ was possessed of sinful propensities is to teach that He himself was a sinner in need of a Saviour."—*Ibid.,* p. 32.

According to this belief, sinful nature involves guilt in the sight of God. Hence, it is absolutely imperative that Christ have no connection with our sinful nature. But how can this be, since Christ had a human mother? Here is one answer: "The substance of Mary was moulded into a perfect nature for our Lord just as in the beginning the Holy Spirit took chaos and made a perfect world."—*Ibid.,* p. 34. In other words, Mary's genetic deficiencies were altered so that she would pass on only a perfect heredity to Christ, completely unlike the heredity we receive from our parents.

Justification

The next step in this "new theology" involves our experience. It reasons this way: Since we are guilty by nature and since we will retain this nature until glorification and since we continue to be guilty after our conversion and since we sin even in the good deeds we do (because selfishness taints our best efforts, and, even in the very act of overcoming sin we may be guilty), therefore, according to this view, we must focus on justification rather than on sanctification. We must look to an imputed righteousness outside of us at all times, since whatever is within us is corrupted by original sin and a depraved heredity.

Thus in this line of thought, the gospel *is* justification, the righteousness of Christ credited to our account. Righteousness by faith becomes justification *only,* while sanctification is basically good advice. This must be so, it is argued, since anything which is corrupted with original sin can never participate in a perfect righteousness by faith. Thus we are forensically, legally righteous, while we are actually inwardly guilty at all times. We must always emphasize Christ's work *for* us rather than the Holy Spirit's work *in* us.

Perfection

Finally, in the "new theology" the basic premise of sin as depraved nature leads to an inevitable conclusion regarding perfection of character. If our essential guilt resides in our nature, the nature with which we were born, and if we retain this nature until death or translation, then it becomes patently clear that there should be no talk of perfection, overcoming as Jesus overcame, or sinlessness in this life. If, in spite of growing spiritually during a lifetime of trusting Jesus more and relying less on our own efforts, we are just as guilty at age sixty as we were at age eighteen, then the words "character perfection" are meaningless and ought to be dropped quickly from our spiritual vocabularies.

Thus the repudiation of the possibility of moral perfection in this life is a necessary corollary to the doctrine of original sin. In this line of thought, the very effort to attain moral perfection results in legalism and a denial of righteousness by faith. Even after the close of probation the characters of God's people will be defective in faith, hope, and love. Since the only meaning of sinlessness is a totally sinless nature, for the "new theology" that will never happen until glorification.

The above few lines summarize the gospel according to one well-developed and carefully articulated system of belief which is found both within and outside Adventism. It is consistent from its presuppositions to its conclusions, and I believe that if you begin with the foundational premises of this system, you must logically end with its conclusions. That is one reason the so-called Reformation theology has become so attractive to many longtime Adventists. So, if we desire to be logical and biblical, are we forced to accept this understanding of the gospel, with other options being both illogical and unbiblical?

I believe that the true gospel, the gospel of Jesus Christ and Paul, is based on different presuppositions and leads to different conclusions. I believe that this is the only gospel that deals adequately with the great cosmic issues in the controversy between God and Satan. I believe that this is the only gospel which will provide security and hope for the Seventh-day Adventist Church and for individuals asking the age-old question, What must I do to inherit eternal life? What follows then, is a short summary of the other way of understanding the gospel promised in the Old Testament and realized in the New.

The Gospel as Defined in Adventism

The basic presupposition of this gospel is that the heart of the cosmic controversy between God and Satan revolves around the issue of free choice and whether Satan has misrepresented God in his damning accusations. God took terrible risks with the universe to protect freedom of choice and to give created beings an opportunity to judge whether He was really what Satan made Him out to be.

Why did God allow the misery of sin? Because of the worthlessness of forced obedience and the necessity of the possibility to sin if righteousness was to be possible. After Adam sinned and lost his freedom of choice, Jesus, "the Lamb slain from the foundation of the world" (Revelation 13:8) volunteered to come to this earth to help clarify these issues and to give mankind a second probation. And the agony of sin will not end until Satan *freely* bows down and confesses Jesus' lordship. This means that the greatest tragedy of the universe is Satan's maligning of God, a tragedy even greater than any sins. Thus the issue to be resolved is how fallen and unfallen beings, will *choose* in the great controversy, either for God or for Satan. This means that the gospel can never be based on predestination of any kind, which essentially bypasses any right of man to choose for or against God. The gospel is built solidly on the foundation of free choice—two very important words in the great controversy between Christ and Satan.

The Nature of Sin

Here again we are led to a decision about the nature of sin. Sin is not basically the way man *is,* but the way man *chooses.* Sin occurs when the mind *consents* to what seems desirable and thus breaks its relationship with God. To talk of guilt in terms of inherited nature is to overlook the important category of responsibility. Not until we have joined our own will to mankind's rebellion against God, not until we have actively entered into opposition to the will of God, does guilt enter the human experience.

Sin is concerned with a man's life, his rebellion against God, his willful disobedience, and the distorted relationship with God which results from his rebellion. Sin is concerned with a man's will rather than with his nature. If responsibility for sin is to have any meaning, it cannot also be affirmed that fallen human nature makes man an inevitable sinner. Inevitability and responsibility are mutually exclusive concepts in the moral sphere. Thus sin is defined as choosing willfully to rebel against God in thought, word, or action. "Whoever knows what is right to do and fails to do it, for him it is sin." James 4:17, RSV. In the New Testament gospel, sin is our willful choice to exercise our fallen, sinful nature in opposition to God's will.

The Human Nature of Christ

Building on this foundation, we move to the nature of Christ—that which He inherited from His ancestors when He became human. If sin is not nature but choice, then Christ could inherit our fallen, sinful nature without thereby becoming a sinner. He remained ever sinless because His conscious choice was always obedience to God, never allowing His inherited nature to control His choices. His inheritance was just the same as our inheritance, with no need to resort to special intervention by God to prevent Jesus from receiving human sinfulness from Mary. "Since therefore the children share in flesh and blood, he [Jesus] himself likewise partook of the same nature. . . . Therefore he had to be made like his brethren in every respect." Hebrews 2:14-17, RSV.

Christ accepted voluntarily the humiliation of descending, not only to the level of unfallen man, but to the level to which man had fallen since Adam sinned. When Jesus was here man obviously was not in Adam's state before the fall, so something far more drastic was needed if the effects of Adam's fall were to be overcome. Christ must descend to the depths to which mankind had fallen through the centuries and in His own person lift mankind from its fallen depths to a new level of life—the life that men and women were once created to live. Jesus stooped from the very heights to the very depths to lift us up.

If Jesus had assumed a perfect human nature untouched by the fall, then He would not have stood side by side with man in his need. If Jesus had assumed unfallen human nature, there would have been a great gulf created by sin. It was *fallen* humanity that He was to represent before God. He stood at the side of fallen sinners to mediate between sinful men and women and a holy God.

If Jesus assumed perfect human nature, He spanned the gulf between God and sinless Adam, but the gulf between God and fallen mankind still needed to be bridged. If, however, Christ shared our fallen, sinful nature, then His mediatorial work bridges the gulf between fallen man and God. Only by entering into our situation in the deepest and fullest sense, identifying Himself fully with us, was He able to be our Saviour. Any other human condition except that of mankind's inherited nature would have been challenged at once by the enemy and would have influenced the thinking of the universe.

It is interesting to note that this understanding of Christ's human condition was the one believed strongly by A. T. Jones and E. J. Waggoner in their righteousness-by-faith messages of 1888, which were endorsed so highly by Ellen White. In fact, this understanding of Christ's life was the accenting power of their messages: the Lord Jesus Christ—loyal to God in sinful flesh.

Justification

From here the gospel message moves to our own personal experience. The gospel is the good news about God's character, that God both forgives and restores. The gospel is (1) God's declaration that we stand righteous in the merits of Christ and (2) God's promise to renovate our sinful lives so that, gradually, we may be restored into His image. The gospel concerns both a legal verdict and a transforming power. Union with Christ is the key to the faith through which justification must take place. The gospel includes justification—a uniting with Christ by faith, on the basis of which we are declared righteous— and sanctification—a growing more like Christ through the enabling power of the Holy Spirit, on the basis of which we are made righteous.

Perfection

Finally, this gospel can speak comfortably and biblically about Christian perfection, which is simply letting God do His full work in us as we depend ever more fully upon Him through faith. This is not extremism in perfection. It is not trying to be good enough to please God or to be saved; it is not removal of our sinful nature; it is not dependence on our internal goodness.

Biblical perfection is total victory over sin, when, through total submission to Christ's power, sin becomes so repulsive that we have no desire to transgress God's will. If sin is our willful choice to rebel against God in thought, word, or action, then sinlessness is our willful choice *not* to rebel against God in thought, word, or action. The purpose of biblical perfection is not primarily to save us, but to honor Christ. It is not the eradication of our sinful nature, but the restoration of that nature through a relationship with Christ. It is not a plateau, but unceasing growth and teachableness. It is not awareness of our inward holiness, but joy in depending on Christ for His mercies and power. It is not being free from temptation, but refusing to yield to temptation. It is not autonomous goodness, but total dependence so that we are finished with rebelling.

This gospel affirms that it is possible to have a sinless character in a sinful nature. The purpose of the gospel is to destroy sin. Thus, becoming morally perfect is the goal, while abiding in Christ is the method. Furthermore, our daily concern is not primarily with the end product, but with our relationship with and our trust in Christ. Only with this understanding of Christian perfection of character does the Seventh-day Adventist message of the second coming carry motivating power. This understanding often demands agonizing with God in prayer. Do we know what it means to wrestle with God as did Jacob? Are our souls drawn out after God with intensity of desire until every power is on the stretch? Do we cling with unyielding faith to "his precious and very great promises, that through these you may escape from the corruption that is in the world because of passion, and become partakers of the divine nature." 2 Peter 1:4, RSV.

Conclusion

These, then, are the two gospels being preached within Adventism. Do you see why these two systems are incompatible? Do you see that compromise between them is impossible, that you must make a choice for your personal faith? I challenge you to study and pray for yourselves, so that you will know what you believe and why, rightly dividing the word of truth. Informed and Spirit-guided decisions must be made that will stand up under the pressures of the last days, and, more important, under the scrutinizing eye of God as He probes our consciences to see whether we make honest decisions or whether we have rationalized and equivocated, seeking the easier way. May the good news be *God's* good news and not man's invention.

THE FRUITAGE OF THE DOCTRINE OF SIN IN THE TWO GOSPELS

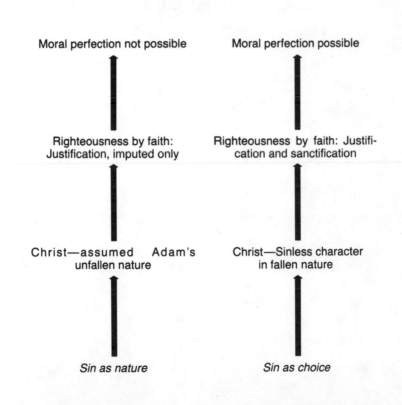

Moral perfection not possible   Moral perfection possible

Righteousness by faith: Justification, imputed only   Righteousness by faith: Justification and sanctification

Christ—assumed Adam's unfallen nature   Christ—Sinless character in fallen nature

Sin as nature   *Sin as choice*

What Is Sin?

Righteousness by faith is probably the most important of all biblical subjects and lies at the foundation of any discussion regarding how men and women are saved. But what is righteousness by faith and how does it relate to the gospel? We have had much controversy within the Seventh-day Adventist Church over these questions. It is highly significant that in serious debate of these issues we are driven back to one subject which seems to lie below all other subjects—the definition of sin.

What is sin? Why are we concerned about a subject which seems so negative? Simply because one's conclusions about righteousness by faith depend on the definition one gives for sin. Why is man guilty? For what reason does God condemn a man? Why does God say that man must die in the fires of hell? What we decide about sin will affect every other decision we make about the nature of righteousness by faith.

Perhaps we have assumed that we know what sin is. It may be helpful to take another look at our assumptions and decide for ourselves what we really mean when we use the word *sin*. We all know that we have sinned, but how? As we said earlier, when we go to a physician, he must discover what is wrong before he can give a proper prescription. Just so, we must know exactly what is wrong with our lives before Jesus Christ can save us from our problems—our sin. We must know the nature of the disease to which the remedy will be applied.

So let us go back and look at the sin that began all of the trouble that we've had in this world. We know that Adam chose sin voluntarily. We know that he became guilty because of his choice. But what about us? Are we guilty because of Adam's sin, because we were born as descendants of Adam? Are we guilty because we have inherited a fallen nature from him? Or are we guilty because we choose to repeat Adam's sin?

Thus we're back to the question of the nature of sin once again. What must the gospel forgive and heal? The basic question which must be resolved is this: What is the nature of sin for which a person is considered guilty, so guilty that he will die in the flames of hell unless God forgives him? What is the nature of *that* sin?

Sin as Nature

Now we must begin with precise definitions. Many definitions of sin have been put forward through the centuries.

One group says that our guilt is the inevitable result of something called original sin. According to this line of thought, original sin does not mean Adam's choice to sin. It means the state in which we are born because of Adam's sin. As a result or because of Adam's sin, we are born sinners. Although the term *original sin* has been used by many theologians, perhaps we need to move away from the term as such and talk about the issues which are behind the term. Sometimes theological terms tend to obscure, rather than to clarify. What does the term really mean?

Original sin can be defined in several ways. Some say that we are guilty because we have inherited sin from Adam. Some say we are guilty, not because we inherit guilt, but because we are born as sons and daughters of

Adam, and thus we are imputed as guilty because of our birth into a fallen race. Thus Adam's guilt is imputed to us.

Another variation says that we are not guilty either because of inheriting sin or because of being imputed as guilty, but because we are born into a separated state. We are born estranged from God. We are born apart from God, and that separation is our guilt. It is that estrangement for which we are guilty. Some even say that we are not personally guilty, but we are born condemned as part of a fallen race.

But the one common denominator through all of these views is that we are guilty or condemned because we are born into the human family. So, however we explain it with these various views, what is being said is that guilt or condemnation is inherited by nature. Our fallen nature is our guilt.

However, even more is being said—and that is, we have *two* kinds of sin in our lives: (1) We are guilty because of our birth as part of this race, and (2) we are also guilty because of our own sins, our own choices, our own acts of rebellion. Both aspects are sin. So although there are two aspects to sin, namely, our birth into a fallen race and our rebellious choices, we are already condemned because of our birth, *before* our choices. This is the bottom line of the term *original sin*. We are guilty or condemned the moment we are born because of Adam's sin.

The implications of this belief are expressed in the following statements. "Sin is declared to exist in the being prior to our own consciousness of it." "There is guilt in evil desires, even when resisted by the will." "Sin is our inherited evil nature and all its fruits."

So you see, according to this definition, sin exists in us *before* choice or even before knowledge. Sin exists in us *before* we can understand and make decisions about right and wrong. Sin resides within us because of our birth into a fallen race.

John Calvin, one of the greatest of systematic theologians, had this to say about sin and guilt. "All of us . . . come into the world tainted with the contagion of sin. . . .We are in God's sight defiled and polluted. . . . The impurity of parents is transmitted to their children. . . . All are originally depraved. . . . *Guilt is from nature.*" (Emphasis supplied by author). Calvin says that the hereditary corruption and depravity of our nature is designated sin by Paul. "Even infants bringing their condemnation with them from their mother's womb suffer . . . for their own defect." And of course this is sinful in the sight of God, for God does not condemn without guilt. "The whole man . . . is so deluged . . . that no part remains exempt from sin, and, therefore, everything which proceeds from him is imputed as sin. . . . Men are born vicious. . . . We are all sinners *by nature.*"—John Calvin, *Institutes of the Christian Religion,* bk. II, ch. 1, #5, 6, 7, 8, 9, 10, 27; emphasis supplied.

You see, this understanding of sin clarifies why the Roman Catholic Church, Martin Luther, and John Calvin all held to the necessity of infant baptism. If, in fact, one is guilty by nature, it is extremely important that one be baptized immediately upon birth to wash this sin away, to be cleansed from this guilt of birth. Infant baptism is extremely important for those who have a problem of original sin. And so Martin Luther and John Calvin argued strenuously for its necessity. Upon birth, children must be baptized immediately and cleansed from the sin which is inherent within them. Both Calvin and Luther were in agreement with and received their understanding of original sin from Augustine.

Luther and Calvin also held the doctrine of predestination, which they also received from Augustine. Augustine believed that God has predestined all men to be either saved or lost. Martin Luther and John Calvin followed in this direction, and they built their doctrine of righteousness by faith upon the presupposition of predestination. Original sin fits in very logically with the doctrine of predestination.

There is still another dimension to the belief that sin is inherent in nature. When Adam sinned, he lost the ability not to sin, so that all that was left for Adam was the ability to sin. Whatever decisions Adam made were sinful decisions. Thus Adam, after his sin, was only able to sin, and we as members of the fallen human race are also only able to sin. In fact, the only thing we can do is sin, and God can only forgive us of our sin.

What I am saying is that this doctrine has many different ways of being expressed. But the basic concept running through all these definitions is that we are born sinners. We are born guilty or condemned. We are guilty or condemned because of being part of the family of Adam.

It might be well to note in passing the reaction of Emil Brunner to this doctrine. "Thus the ecclesiastical doctrine, which is based entirely upon the idea of the fall of Adam, and the transference of his sin to the succeeding generations, is following a method which is in no sense Biblical. Even that passage, Rom. 5:12 ff. which seems to be an exception, and has been regarded as the *locus classicus* of Christian theology from the time of Augustine, cannot be regarded as supporting this Augustinian view, which was followed by succeeding generations. For here Paul is not trying to explain what sin is; indeed, there is really nothing in Rom. 5 which describes the nature of sin." "The theory of Original Sin which has been the standard one for the Christian doctrine of man, from the time of St. Augustine, is completely foreign to the thought of the Bible." "Sin is first of all to be understood as an act, namely as a 'fall', as an active break with the divine beginning, as an active departure from the divine order. . . . Sin is an *act*—that is the first thing to say about sin. Only as a second point we can say: this act is always, at the same time, a *state,* an existence in action, a state in which one cannot do otherwise, a state of slavery."—Emil Brunner, *The Christian Doctrine of Creation and Redemption,* pp. 98, 99, 103, 109.

I would like to suggest that the evidence supporting the doctrine of original sin, in whatever way it is explained, whether by inheritance or by imputation or by separation, is not a clear biblical teaching as some have thought it to be. There is at least another way of understanding the texts that are used in support of this view of original sin.

Sin as Choice

Let us now focus on the second definition of sin, namely, sin as choice. In this definition, we are saying many of the same things that have been stated in the various definitions of original sin.

We believe that in Adam's original nature nothing led him to rebel against God. No desires led him away from God's will. For Adam it was natural to do right, and it was very unnatural to do wrong. But with the fall, something changed in Adam's very nature, in the innermost part of his being. The fall brought to Adam a *bent* to evil. His nature was now distorted and twisted, and Adam now *wanted* to do what he had hated to do before, namely, to rebel against God. Now, for Adam, it was natural to sin. Now, it was unnatural to do right.

So when we say that we inherit a fallen nature from Adam, we must understand its full significance. We do inherit badness, weakness, and corruption from Adam. We have the same desires that Adam had in his sinful state. We desire to do wrong; we desire to rebel against God. It is hard for us to do right. It is more natural to do wrong. I think if we're honest with ourselves, we will admit that we are our own tempters all too often. We really do not need Satan to follow us around and tempt us with all sorts of ideas, because we are well able to tempt ourselves. Our own natures lead us astray. Selfishness seems to be at the root of our lives, prompting us to do things we know we shouldn't do. So we do inherit negative tendencies from Adam, which lead us to do wrong.

The one difference in this definition from the previous definition of sin is that we do not inherit guilt or condemnation. We do inherit everything that Adam could pass on. We inherit all of the leanings, all of the tendencies, all of the desires, and we are born in a way that God did not really intend for man to be born. But this definition says that personal sin comes through choice; sin, itself, is not inherited. Guilt, then, is not by nature; but when we choose to rebel against the light and known duty, *then* we become guilty. We must choose to make Adam's decision, the decision to rebel against God, and *then* we are guilty.

We must admit that sinful nature makes it easier to sin—to make sinful choices. But the point that I would like to stress is that we are guilty *when* we make those choices, not *before* we make them. Therefore, I believe that we must carefully distinguish between the concepts of evil and guilt.

We have outlined the two basic definitions of sin. Depending upon which definition we choose to believe, the issues of righteousness by faith will be colored differently. The decisions we make about justification and sanctification will be different, depending upon the decision we make about the nature of sin.

Evil and Guilt

If we want to define sin as choice, we must make a distinction between evil and guilt. There is much evil in the world today, even in the animal world. But we don't impute guilt to all of the evil that is apparent in our world today.

One of my favorite illustrations is that of the common household pet, the cat. We enjoy cats that snuggle up in our laps or on our feet, who like to be petted, who come for their dish of warm milk. But sometimes we forget that there is another side to our household pets. Have you noticed that cats are not merciful with mice that they have caught for their next meal? When they are able to catch a mouse, they do not quickly put it out of its misery, but they play with the mouse. They, in fact, torture the mouse, until the mouse finds it physically impossible to run away and finally gives up.

What would we do to a human being who would torture an animal or a human being in that same way? We would consider him guilty of the most heinous of crimes and would probably lock him up for the rest of his life. But what do we do with the animal who has done that—with our cat? We say that it is part of the way life is. It is not good that the mouse suffers, but the cat is not guilty, either. Thus we see some acts as evil but part of the natural results of sin, and other acts as evil for which a person may be considered guilty.

Now, to bring this to the human level. If we are pounding a post and ask a friend to hold that post so that we'll be better able to drive it, we might miss the post and hit our friend's thumb. That thumb will hurt, be discolored, and take some time to heal, but our friend will probably not accuse us of any personal guilt. He will treat it as an unfortunate accident.

Let us take it one step further to make the point. If a small child plays with a gun and shoots his older brother or sister, we would take that gun away from the child and simply make sure that we locked up our firearms better in the future. We would not condemn or judge that child as guilty. But if a twenty-year-old takes that same gun and shoots someone, we would immediately ask some questions beginning with Why? We would want to know, first of all, whether he is guilty of malice.

So there is a difference between the concepts of evil and guilt. The word *evil* simply means that which is bad, negative, or wrong, the *results* of sin in a cursed world. Guilt applies to moral responsibility for evil thoughts or acts.

What I'm saying is that trees and animals are full of sin and evil, but they are not condemned nor are they redeemed by God, for they have no knowledge of moral values. Only man has a knowledge of moral values, and because of this knowledge he is condemned as guilty for any evil acts. If we are to believe that sin is by choice, we must make a crucial distinction between evil and guilt. Guilt demands prior knowledge and willful rebellion. I am suggesting that God's condemnation is *always* based upon man's prior knowledge. James said it clearly, "Whoever knows what is right to do and fails to do it, for him it is sin." Chapter 4:17, RSV.

Result and Penalty

Now we must try to substantiate the hypothesis that there is a difference between the concepts of evil and guilt. In Genesis 2:17 a distinct and clear penalty is given for rebelling against God. Adam was told by God, "Of the tree of the knowledge of good and evil, thou shalt not eat of it: for in the day that thou eatest thereof thou shalt surely die." We've been puzzled about that verse, because it is just as clear that when Adam did eat of the fruit which Eve gave to him, he didn't die that day.

So we have sometimes said, Well, he began to die. But the Hebrew simply says, "In the day that thou eatest thereof, dying, thou shalt die." The translation, "In the day that thou eatest thereof thou shalt surely die," is a good one. Then why didn't Adam die that day? "Why was not the death penalty at once enforced in his case? Because a ransom was found. God's only begotten Son volunteered to take the sin of man upon himself, and to make an atonement for the fallen race."—Ellen G. White Comments, *S.D.A. Bible Commentary*, vol. 1, p. 1082.

"The instant man accepted the temptations of Satan, and did the very things God had said he should not do, Christ, the Son of God, stood between the living and the dead, saying, 'Let the punishment fall on Me. I will stand in man's place. He shall have another chance.' "—*Ibid.*, p. 1085. "As soon as there was sin, there was a Saviour. . . . As soon as Adam sinned, the Son of God presented Himself as surety for the human race, with just as much power to avert the doom pronounced upon the guilty as when He died upon the cross of Calvary."—*Ibid.*, p. 1084.

Why didn't Adam die that day? Because the Substitute was placed between the penalty of death and Adam that day. Jesus Christ took Adam's place that very day. Perhaps this helps us to understand Revelation 13:8, where the Lamb is said to be slain from the foundation of the world. As man's surety, Jesus, in effect, did pay the penalty that day, stepping between Adam and the death penalty on that day.

Very soon thereafter Adam offered the first animal sacrifice which meant for him that the Son of God would die in his place. Thus the penalty for Adam's sin was paid immediately by Jesus Christ. Jesus Christ took Adam's place immediately.

But will Adam ever pay that penalty? Will Adam ever die to pay for his sin? Why did Adam die 930 years later? Did he ever pay the penalty? Or did he die simply as the *result* of sin's inherent consequences?

In fact, we're told that his death was a blessing, because he had endured so much agony knowing that his sin had caused all of the sin and pain and suffering that he had witnessed for 900 years. Thus his death was actually a relief. This death, the natural death that Adam died, was the *result* of sin, rather than the *penalty* of sin. The penalty had been paid by Jesus Christ. Adam had offered the lamb, showing that he understood that the death penalty had been paid. But the curse—sin's inherent consequences—remained.

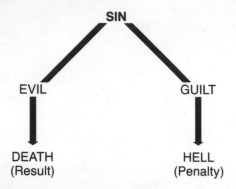

This means that we must divide the basic idea of sin into two separate columns. The column on the left side is labeled EVIL, which includes all the things which *inherently result* from sin, and all of this evil leads to death. But this death Jesus called a sleep, which is not the final end for man. Thus evil and its results lead to death and suffering and all of the negative things we see around us.

The column on the right is labeled GUILT. And this column leads to the second death, or hell, which is the *penalty* for sin. So we really have two consequences of sin. We have the curse—the inherent results of sin—that human beings, animals, and all nature generally experience which leads to death, the first death. On the other side, we have guilt, which leads to the penalty for sin, the second death, which has been paid by Jesus Christ. If we choose to accept Jesus Christ's salvation, we will never die the second death.

Now it is true that the atonement covers both of these consequences of sin. But I would suggest that the atonement must deal with *guilt* by *forgiving* it and with *evil results* by *recreating* and *restoring* what the curse of sin has done. The atonement works toward restoring all things to God's original plan, but it doesn't *forgive* those areas found in the left column. It only forgives those areas on the guilt side—that is, it can only forgive the penalty of sin.

Thus the terms *justification, forgiveness, salvation,* the *gospel,* and *righteousness* and *sanctification* apply particularly to those issues in the right-hand column, those issues having to do with guilt, penalty, and hell. What I'm suggesting is that there is a basic difference between the *result* of sin and the *penalty* of sin. There is a basic difference between the first death and the second death, and the issues of condemnation and salvation pertain particularly to guilt and its penalty. It is on these areas that we must focus when we speak about righteousness by faith.

Now, let's look at some texts in the New Testament to see if we have further evidence for this distinction. In Luke 13:1-5, Jesus tells a story to drive home a lesson. Luke says some present had told Jesus of the Galileans whose blood had been mingled with their sacrifices. In other words, they had been killed. "And Jesus answering said unto them, Suppose ye that these Galileans were sinners above all the Galileans, because they suffered such things? I tell you, Nay: but, except ye repent, ye shall all likewise perish. Or those eighteen, upon whom the tower in Siloam fell, and slew them, think ye that they were sinners above all men that dwelt in Jerusalem? I tell you, Nay: but, except ye repent, ye shall all likewise perish."

Here we see that the death of the Galileans was not the direct result of their sin. Jesus was saying that these Galileans and the ones upon whom the tower fell were not more guilty than others because of their death. Here it is clear that the first death that they died was not tied directly to their guilt.

In John 9:1-3, the disciples, seeing a blind man, asked Christ, "Who did sin, this man, or his parents, that he was born blind? Jesus answered, Neither hath this man sinned, nor his parents: but that the works of God should be made manifest in him." Once again Jesus was saying that his blindness, the curse with which he was afflicted, was not the result of any personal sin but was caused by an inherited weakness. Jesus is here making a distinction between personal guilt and the inherent effects or results of sin.

Another important text is John 5:24, 25. Unless we understand this distinction we are making in this chapter, we may have Jesus contradicting Himself in this passage. "Verily, verily, I say unto you, He that heareth my word, and believeth on him that sent me, hath everlasting life, and shall not come into condemnation; but is passed from death unto life."

Jesus is saying that right now, today, if we believe, we have everlasting life. Right now, we are passed from death to life. But He continues by saying, "Verily, verily, I say unto you, The hour is coming, and now is, when the dead shall hear the voice of the Son of God: and they that hear shall live." In verse 24 we are free from death; we have everlasting life now. In verse 25 those who have died shall hear the voice of the Son of God in the resurrection to come. Unless we make this distinction between the first death and the second death, we find ourselves in a rather hopeless contradiction.

Jesus is saying that we have eternal life today in Him. We are freed from the penalty of guilt. We have been delivered, and we will never die the second death—sin's penalty. Nevertheless, except for those who will be translated, we will die the death which is called a sleep (such as in the case of Lazarus). Later we will hear the voice of the Son of God and rise from the sleep of the first death. So even those who are forgiven and are given eternal life will still die as the *result* of the curse of Adam's sin. We must die because we are in a world which is dying. The first death cannot be the penalty for sin, since those who possess eternal life will also die the first death. Simply put—eternal life means no second death, which is the penalty for sin. Another text which expresses this thought very clearly is 1 John 5:12, 13, in which we are said to have life in Christ now, today, and yet we know that we will die.

So I think that we have good scriptural evidence that there are two different consequences of sin: (1) the curse of sin, which leads to the first death, and (2) the penalty of sin, which leads to the second death.

Light and Choice

Is it really true that guilt is the result of one's personal choice and not a result of our birth as children of Adam? Can we substantiate from the Bible that sin and guilt come from choice, not from the fact we are born into the human family beset with the inherent results of sin? Let's look at the biblical evidence.

In Romans 7:7-9, Paul speaks about the law and our relationship to it. Paul says, "I had not known sin, but by the law: for I had not known lust, except the law had said, Thou shalt not covet. . . . For without the law sin was dead. For I was alive without the law once: but when the commandment came, sin revived, and I died." Here Paul says that we know what sin is because the law tells us, and if we did not know about the law we would really not have any knowledge or understanding of sin. He even goes so far as to say that without the law, sin is dead. Thus we sin when we know what God's will is. We sin when we understand and choose against God.

In John 15:22, 24 Jesus, speaking to His disciples just before His death, says, "If I had not come and spoken unto them, they had not had sin: but now they have no cloak for their sin." "If I had not done among them the works which none other man did, they had not had sin: but now they have both seen and hated both me and my Father."

Because of what people now knew about Jesus and what He had done, they were responsible for the way they related to Him. Because of His coming and their knowledge, they were guilty if they rejected Him.

In John 9:41, Jesus is responding to some of the criticisms of the Pharisees, and He says, "If ye were blind, ye should have no sin: but now ye say, We see; therefore your sin remaineth." That is, if you were truly blind, if you really didn't know, you wouldn't be guilty of sin. But you say, we see; therefore you are guilty of sin.

Doesn't it seem clear that sin and guilt are tied closely to knowledge and understanding and light? Perhaps the distinguishing factor between the two columns we used earlier (which helped to differentiate evil from guilt) is the biblical term *light*. What changes evil into guilt is light or knowledge or understanding—and the choices made upon the basis of that new light or understanding.

In the book of James, some light is shed on this problem. In James 4:17, James says, "Therefore to him that knoweth to do good, and doeth it not, to him it is sin." To the one who knows what is right and fails to do it, to that person, it is sin. Once again knowledge and guilt are tied closely together. James 1:15 says, "When lust [desire] hath conceived, it bringeth forth sin: and sin, when it is finished, bringeth forth death." Here we see a development from lust, or desire, to actual sin. Sin is not necessarily within the desire itself. Sin is what is produced by that desire. Sin is the result of yielding to that desire.

In the Old Testament, Ezekiel 18:2-4 refers to a proverb used by the children of Israel. "What mean ye, that ye use this proverb concerning the land of Israel, saying, The fathers have eaten sour grapes, and the children's teeth are set on edge? As I live, saith the Lord God, ye shall not have occasion any more to use this proverb in Israel. Behold, all souls are mine; as the soul of the father, so also the soul of the son is mine: the soul that sinneth, it shall die." In verse 20, Ezekiel reemphasizes this biblical principle: "The soul that sinneth, it shall die. The son shall not bear the iniquity of the father, neither shall the father bear the iniquity of the son." Individual responsibility for individual choices—individual freedom of choice.

Now what does God do about those who are doing wrong *ignorantly*, who are out of harmony with the will of God? How does He handle such situations? Paul says in Acts 17:30: "The times of this ignorance God winked at; but now commandeth all men everywhere to repent." In times of ignorance, men are doing evil things. They are doing things which are out of harmony with the will of God. They are breaking God's law and God's will. How does God handle that problem? What does He do about that? According to this verse, He "winks at," or overlooks, the times of ignorance. He does not forgive, but He overlooks. But whenever light and knowledge come, evil then becomes guilt. And for that sin done in the face of knowledge, the sinner must repent and seek forgiveness.

Our Lord's statement in Matthew 11:21-24 is made a little clearer with this understanding: "If the mighty works, which were done in you [Bethsaida], had been done in Tyre and Sidon, they would have repented long ago in sackcloth and ashes. But I say unto you, It shall be more tolerable for Tyre and Sidon at the day of judgment, than for you. . . . If the mighty works, which have been done in thee [Capernaum], had been done in Sodom, it would have remained until this day. But I say unto you, That it shall be more tolerable for the land of Sodom in the day of judgment, than for thee."

Now in terms of quantity of evil works, I am sure that Sodom far outstripped Capernaum. But the condemnation was heavier upon Capernaum. Why? Capernaum had more light. They had the privilege of accepting Jesus Himself. Of course Sodom had done evil things, but many of those evil things had been done in lesser light. They did not understand God's way, and Lot was not a very good representative of the way of God for them. Because of their ignorance they were not as guilty as were the people of Capernaum, who had rejected greater light. So Capernaum was more guilty than Sodom, because they had more light; their choices were based on a more complete knowledge. Psalm 87:4-6 suggests that the Lord will take note of where a man is born, of where a man is brought up. He will make judgments on the basis of where a man is, what background he has had, how much understanding he has had of God's will.

Ellen White makes some important statements on the subject of sin and guilt. "It is inevitable that children should suffer from the consequences of parental wrongdoing, but they are not punished for the parents' guilt, except as they participate in their sins. . . . By inheritance and example the sons become partakers of the father's sin. Wrong tendencies, perverted appetites, and debased morals, as well as physical disease and degeneracy, are transmitted as a legacy from father to son, to the third and fourth generation."—*Patriarchs and Prophets,* p. 306.

Please note what is transmitted as a result of Adam's sin. Wrong tendencies, perverted appetites, even debased morals, as well as physical disease and degeneracy. These are all part of what we receive from our parents and our ancestors. But let us note also that very important statement that children "are not punished for the parents' guilt, except as they participate in their sins." This is rather conclusive evidence for the doctrine that sin and guilt arise out of choice in the face of sufficient knowledge regarding right and wrong.

"We shall not be held accountable for the light that has not reached our perception, but for that which we have resisted and refused. A man could not apprehend the truth which had never been presented to him, and therefore could not be condemned for light he had never had."—Ellen G. White Comments, *S.D.A. Bible Commentary,* vol. 5, p. 1145. Personal guilt is charged only on the basis of light and knowledge. We are not condemned because we do things which are evil or wrong unless we understand to some degree that such things are wrong. "None will be condemned for not heeding light and knowledge that they never had."—*Ibid.* It seems clear that she is basing condemnation upon understanding, upon willful decisions. "Light makes manifest and reproves the errors that were concealed in darkness; and as light comes, the life and character of men must change correspondingly, to be in harmony with it. Sins that were once sins of ignorance, because of the blindness of the mind, can no more be indulged in without incurring guilt."—*Gospel Workers,* p. 162. Once we know that our acts are wrong, we become guilty if we keep on indulging in those sins. But before we knew, we were not guilty. After we understand, we are guilty. Guilt is thus tied to choice and to knowledge.

"There were still many among the Jews who were ignorant of the character and the work of Christ [after the time of Jesus, just before the destruction of Jerusalem]. And the children had not enjoyed the opportunities or received the light which their parents had spurned. . . . The children were not condemned for the sins of the parents; but when, with a knowledge of all the light given to their parents, the children rejected the additional light granted to themselves, they became partakers of the parents' sins, and filled up the measure of their iniquity."—*The Great Controversy,* pp. 27, 28. Because of personal involvement and personal understanding, guilt was imputed.

"The sin of evilspeaking begins with the cherishing of evil thoughts. . . . An impure thought *tolerated,* an unholy desire *cherished,* and the soul is contaminated, its integrity compromised."—*Testimonies,* vol. 5, p. 177; emphasis supplied. Please note the difference. It is the *toleration* of the impure thought, it is the *cherishing* of the unholy desire that constitutes sin and contamination. It is not the thought or the desire itself. It is not right to say that there is sin in the desire to sin if that desire is instantly repulsed. "Every unholy thought must be *instantly repelled.*" "No man can be forced to transgress. *His own consent* must first be gained; the soul must *purpose* the sinful act before passion can dominate over reason or iniquity triumph over conscience. Temptation, however strong, is never an excuse for sin."—*Ibid.;* emphasis supplied. The inclinations of the natural heart are not sin in themselves until they are cherished, until they are wanted; in consenting to evil thoughts we cross the boundary between evil and guilt. The inclination is evil, but we are not guilty for that inclination until we choose to act upon it.

"If light come, and that light is set aside or rejected, then comes condemnation and the frown of God; but before the light comes, there is no sin, for there is no light for them to reject."—*Ibid.,* vol. 1, p. 116. Thus, it seems very clear that sin is tied closely to knowledge and to understanding.

"There are thoughts and feelings suggested and aroused by Satan that annoy even the best of men; but if they are not cherished, if they are repulsed as hateful, the soul is not contaminated with guilt, and no other is defiled by their influence."—*Review and Herald,* March 27, 1888. Those thoughts and feelings, if not cherished, will not contaminate with guilt. The thoughts and feelings are wrong. They are there because of the evil in the world and because of a nature we have that's fallen. But they are not contaminating unless we choose to cherish them or to act them out.

In *Counsels on Health,* page 81, Ellen White notes that

using tobacco injures the body, but God is merciful to those who use it in ignorance. Only after light comes to them are they considered guilty for their use of tobacco. Now tobacco will have its negative effects. It may even lead to cancer, but until light comes, guilt is not imputed. Contracting cancer does not mean, necessarily, that the person is guilty and has sinned against the light of truth.

In conclusion, I believe that guilt resides only within those higher faculties responsible for choosing evil, not in the lower faculties which suffer the effects of natural law and are a part of the earth's cycle of sin. Guilt cannot reside in an amoral natural world but only in man who is responsible for the perversions of moral law. Guilt does not attach itself to man's animal faculties, but to those moral faculties involved in exercising the power of choice.

Sin, at its root, is self-love. Thus sin is determined by motive rather than by acts. It is the choice to put self first, whatever form that takes. Sin is the choice to separate from God by putting self first. It is the choice to cherish evil. It is the choice to remain ignorant of God's will. It is the choice to be careless of one's abilities and responsibilities.

At the foundation of the theological divisions among Adventists on the question of righteousness by faith lie differing beliefs on the nature of sin and guilt. The real debate is over the nature of sin. This question must be clearly answered: Why are we guilty and for what must we be forgiven?

The answer we give to this question directly affects our perception of the way Christ came to this earth. What nature did Christ take? What powers did He use? How did He overcome sin? These questions will receive different answers, depending on one's conclusions regarding the nature of sin.

How Did Christ Live?

This subject has aroused much discussion over the past few years. The purpose of this chapter is to address the question, How did Jesus come to this earth and how did he live as a man? We must let the evidence speak to us so that we can understand what God is saying about His Son, Jesus Christ, and what the Son is saying about the Father.

In discussing the nature of sin, I suggested that if one believes that sin and guilt come as the result of nature, certain conclusions relative to righteousness by faith would follow. In this chapter we will face the first of those conclusions. If one believes that sin comes by nature, that man is guilty or condemned because of the nature with which he is born (either by inheritance or by imputation or by separation from God at birth), then it is absolutely necessary that Jesus Christ should not be born the way we are. If He were born exactly as we are, inheriting guilt or imputed as guilty or separated from God, then He would be guilty and could not be our Saviour, for our Saviour must be sinless. If one takes the position that sin is by nature and we are guilty or condemned because of that nature, then one *must* take the position that Jesus Christ took Adam's nature *before* the fall. So the decision made about the nature of sin predetermines the decision made about the way Jesus Christ was born.

On the other hand, if one takes the position that we

inherit tendencies that are evil and corrupt, that our fallen nature tends to move us in a wrong direction, but we are not guilty because of that nature until we choose to exercise that nature in rebellion against God, then the possibility exists that Jesus could have been born in the same way you and I are born. He could have received the same inheritance without choosing to yield to that nature in rebellion against God. Only with the understanding of sin as choice does this option remain open. So it does make a crucial difference whether we believe that sin is by nature or by choice, because that will determine the conclusions we will draw regarding the humanity of Jesus Christ.

What kind of a man was Jesus Christ? What nature did He take? How was He like us, and how was He different from us? If we believe that sin is by choice, then we can allow the evidence to speak for itself. Was Jesus Christ born with a fallen nature or an unfallen nature? Let us go to the evidence to see what the Bible and spirit of prophecy teach about Jesus Christ and His human nature.

Of What Did Jesus Empty Himself?

One place to start is Philippians 2, where Paul describes Jesus becoming a man. This chapter describes the descent of Jesus Christ to this earth and His ascent back to heaven. Verse 6 says, "Who, being in very nature God, did not consider equality with God something to be grasped." NIV. This verse expresses Jesus' equality with God the Father before coming to this earth—His preincarnation state. He did not have to grasp for equality with God because He was God.

Verse 7 describes the incarnation. "But made himself nothing, taking the very nature of a servant, being made in human likeness." NIV. Now the Greek word that is translated "made himself of no reputation" in the King James Version, really means "emptied himself." In order to become a man, Jesus must empty Himself of certain divine qualities which He exercised freely in His preincarnation state as God.

First of all, He had to lay aside His omnipotence. If Jesus was truly going to live as a man and act as a man, He could not act as an all-powerful God. He must act in a way that is possible for man to act. In John 5:30, Jesus describes His relationship to the Father. "I can of mine own self do nothing: as I hear, I judge: and my judgment is just; because I seek not mine own will, but the will of the Father which hath sent me."

"I can of mine own self do nothing" is not a statement that Jesus would have made before His incarnation. God says that He does all things as He wills. Jesus is saying something here which God would not be expected to say. In John 14:10-12 He adds, "The Father that dwelleth in me, he doeth the works. . . . He that believeth on me, the works that I do shall he do also; and greater works than these shall he do." Once again, this is not typical of God. God is not dependent upon anyone. Only in a man's situation do we speak of dependency. This suggests that Jesus voluntarily suspended the exercise of His power.

When Jesus was sleeping in the boat during the storm on the sea of Galilee, "He rested not in the possession of almighty power. It was not as the 'Master of earth and sea and sky' that He reposed in quiet. That power He had laid down, and He says, 'I can of Mine own self do nothing.'. . . He trusted in the Father's might. It was in faith—faith in God's love and care—that Jesus rested, and the power of that word which stilled the storm was the power of God."—*The Desire of Ages,* p. 336. So Jesus did not use His own power in His miracles. He depended upon His Father's power. In the healing of the paralytic, God gave His Son power to perform that miracle. He also gave His Son power to perform all His other miracles. See *Testimo-*

nies, vol. 8, p. 202. Only at His resurrection was that power restored to Him, when His own deity raised His sleeping humanity from the grave.

Jesus also left behind the memory of His pre-existence. Luke 2:52 says that Jesus grew in wisdom and in stature. To grow in wisdom, one must be lacking in wisdom and must learn. Therefore Jesus, as a man could not have been omniscient, knowing all things, or learning would have been impossible. "The very words which He Himself had spoken to Moses for Israel He was now taught at His mother's knee." "He gained knowledge as we may do. . . . He who had made all things studied the lessons which His own hand had written in earth and sea and sky."— *The Desire of Ages,* p. 70. Gradually He learned more about God and salvation and the issues of the gospel. "The mystery of His mission was opening to the Saviour."—*Ibid.,* p. 78. Gradually He became aware of who He was and what He was to do.

This means that He did not remember what He knew before He came to earth. It is very clear that He knew all things before He came down. "Before He came to earth, the plan lay out before Him, perfect in all its details. But as He walked among men, He was guided, step by step, by the Father's will."—*Ibid.,* p. 147. Before He came to earth, He knew the whole scope of what would happen as the plan of salvation would unfold. But living on earth He did not know what He knew before He came down. On earth, He was guided by the Father's will.

In Mark 13:32, Jesus says, "Of that day and that hour [the second coming] knoweth no man, no not the angels which are in heaven, neither the Son, but the Father." While He was on earth, He did not know when He would be coming back, because the Father had not revealed that to Him. The Father had revealed many other things that were necessary for Jesus to know, but the Father had not revealed the time of Jesus' second coming. During His life on earth, Jesus did not know the future, except as the Father revealed the future to Him.

"Christ in His life on earth made no plans for Himself. He accepted God's plans for Him, and day by day the Father unfolded His plans."—*The Ministry of Healing*, p. 479. "The Saviour could not see through the portals of the tomb. Hope did not present to Him His coming forth from the grave a conqueror, or tell Him of the Father's acceptance of the sacrifice."—*The Desire of Ages*, p. 753. Just before His death, Jesus did not know for sure that He would live again. Earlier He had said that He would, because His Father had revealed that to Him. But now, bearing the whole weight of sin, He was not certain that He would ever come up from the grave again or that the Father would even accept His sacrifice, because sin was such a terrible burden to bear. Perhaps it is important for us to note right here that Jesus died not knowing for sure, but willing to trust His Father. This is what the atonement really cost. Jesus feared the possibility that the separation would be eternal.

It is clear that Jesus left behind His omniscience, knowing what God knows, when He came to this earth. He would have to, if He was to live as a man. Obviously Jesus also had to leave behind His omnipresence. He, as a man, was in one place at one time. He also had to leave behind His glory. Isaiah 53:2 says that there was nothing special about His appearance. He laid aside the glory that was His so He could live as a man.

In summary, Jesus laid aside several aspects of His deity. He could not use those aspects of His deity which make Him God. He must live as a man among men. The quiescence of His deity means that His deity rested inactive during Jesus' life as a man. His deity shared the risk of failure and eternal loss, but it was not permitted to do anything to prevent such a consequence. It was the man Jesus who made decisions and who acted. That is the tremendous risk of the incarnation.

While it is correct to say that Jesus did not cease to be God when He became man, Jesus laid aside those attributes which made Him God, so that He could live as a man. God cannot be tempted with evil, according to James 1, and Jesus certainly was tempted by Satan with evil. Therefore, in the plan of salvation it was essential that Jesus should live as a man, with only the abilities natural to man.

Jesus Took Our Fallen Nature

Much debate has centered on whether Jesus took our fallen nature or Adam's nature before the fall. Even though this may seem like a speculative point, it really has tremendous implications for the kind of life we should live day by day. So let us examine the evidence.

Romans 8:3 is one of the classic statements about Jesus becoming man. "What the law could not do, in that it was weak through the flesh, God sending his own Son in the likeness of sinful flesh, and for sin, condemned sin in the flesh." What exactly does it mean to be in the "likeness of sinful flesh"? We have heard that likeness does not mean sameness.

We have already studied some of the biblical evidence regarding the real humanity of Jesus. He emptied Himself of those things which characterized Him as God. Philippians 2:7 says, "And took upon him the form of a servant, and was made in the *likeness* of men." The same Greek word is used in both texts. In Romans 8:3 it is the "*likeness* of sinful flesh." Emphases supplied. I think all would agree that when Jesus Christ came down to this earth He became a real man. In fact, Docetism, one of the earliest heresies of the Christian church, taught that Jesus did not really become a man, but just appeared to be man. They believed that anything material was evil and therefore Jesus couldn't have taken a physical body.

It was in response to that heresy that John said (1 John 4:2) we must believe that Jesus Christ did come in the flesh—that He was a real human being.

Now, if we want to understand that in Philippians 2:7 the likeness of men means "actually" man, not just "similar to" man, then what must we say about Romans 8:3, where we find the expression, "likeness of sinful flesh"? Did Jesus just look as if He had sinful flesh, or did He *actually* have sinful flesh? The *Expositors Greek Testament* comments on Romans 8:3, 4. "But the emphasis . . . is on Christ's likeness to us, not His unlikeness; . . . what he [Paul] means by it is that God sent His Son in that nature which in us is identified with sin. . . . The flesh . . . in which sin had reigned was also that [flesh] in which God's condemnation of sin was executed." "The flesh meant is our corrupt human nature."—*Expositors Greek Testament* (Grand Rapids, Mich: Wm. B. Eerdmans Pub. Co.) 2:645, 646. It would seem that if we are to interpret likeness in Philippians 2:7 as our actual human nature, then we must interpret likeness in Romans 8:3 as actual sinful flesh.

What did Ellen White believe on this point? Perhaps her most definitive statement is found in *The Desire of Ages.* "It would have been an almost infinite humiliation for the Son of God to take man's nature, even when Adam stood in his innocence in Eden. But Jesus accepted humanity when the race had been weakened by four thousand years of sin. Like every child of Adam He accepted the results of the working of the great law of heredity. What these results were is shown in the history of His earthly ancestors. He came with such a heredity to share our sorrows and temptations, and to give us the example of a sinless life."—Page 49.

We here have substantial information about how and why Jesus became man. "Jesus accepted humanity when the race had been weakened by four thousand years of sin." How did He accept that humanity?

"Like every child of Adam He accepted the results of the working of the great law of heredity." The logical questions follow: How does that law work? What are the results of the working of that law? The next sentence helps to clarify. "What these results were is shown in the history of His earthly ancestors." We know well some of His earthly ancestors. David and Rahab were two of His earthly ancestors. What did they inherit? I think we know the answer to that question. The next sentence says, "He [Jesus] came with such a heredity." Jesus came with the heredity that *David* had! David was his earthly ancestor. Jesus accepted the working of the great law of heredity in the same way His ancestors did. This statement alone is a strong affirmation stating that the way we are born is the way Jesus was born, in terms of heredity.

Perhaps it will help to know exactly what is meant by inheritance. "Both parents transmit their own characteristics, mental and physical, their dispositions and appetites, to their children."—*Patriarchs and Prophets,* p. 561. "Wrong tendencies, perverted appetites, and debased morals, as well as physical disease and degeneracy, are transmitted as a legacy from father to son."—*Ibid.,* p. 306. "There are those who have inherited peculiar tempers and dispositions."—*Testimonies,* vol. 9, p. 222. "He [the father] transmits irritable tempers, polluted blood, enfeebled intellects, and weak morals to his children."—*Ibid.,* vol. 4, pp. 30, 31. "Parents may have transmitted to their children tendencies to appetite and passion."—*Ibid.,* vol. 3, p. 567. "Wrong traits of character received by birth. . ."—*Ibid.,* vol. 5, p. 419. "It will be well to remember that tendencies of character are transmitted from parents to children."—*Ibid.,* vol. 4, p. 439. "While Adam was created sinless, in the likeness of God, Seth, like Cain, inherited the fallen nature of his parents."—*Patriarchs and Prophets,* p. 80.

If it is clear that we as individuals inherit characteristics and tendencies and traits of character in the fallen nature we receive from our parents, and if Jesus accepted the working of the great law of heredity, I believe that the only possible conclusion is that Jesus inherited fallen nature. If *we* inherit fallen nature, and *He* accepted the results of the working of the great law of heredity, then what must He have inherited? No evidence exists to suggest that Jesus inherited only the physical results of the fall, such as hunger, weakness, thirst, and mortality, but that He did not inherit dispositional traits. These areas cannot be separated. If the law of heredity was operative, it was operative totally. If we receive traits of character from our parents, then Jesus received traits of character from His mother, for she was a fully human mother. If we do not believe that she was immaculately conceived, then we believe that she had the same fallen nature that any human being possesses.

In Harry Johnson's study on the humanity of Jesus Christ, he made this statement: "The New Testament supports the theory that Jesus was born into humanity and took full human nature from Mary, and the obvious deduction is that part of this heredity was 'fallen human nature.' There is no evidence to suggest that the chain of heredity was broken between Mary and Jesus." This is the crucial point. There is no evidence that the chain of heredity was broken. The inheritance of Jesus was the same as our inheritance.

Harry Johnson continues, "The birth of Jesus means that He entered fully into our human situation, and that He came into human nature as it was because of the Fall. ... The burden of proof must lie with those who accept the doctrine of an 'inherited weakness,' and yet maintain that Jesus took a real humanity from His mother without inheriting the results of the Fall."—*The Humanity of the Saviour* (London: The Epworth Press, 1962), pp. 44, 45. The burden of proof lies with those who want to say that there was an interference with the heredity which Mary passed on to Jesus. The evidence from the Bible and the spirit of prophesy indicates that His inheritance was the same as our inheritance.

When Jesus was assailed by the tempter, things were not the same as they were with Adam. "For four thousand years the race had been decreasing in physical strength, in mental power, and in moral worth; and Christ took upon Him the infirmities of degenerate humanity."—*The Desire of Ages,* p. 117. In *Selected Messages,* bk. 1, pp. 267, 268, we find virtually the same thing. "Having taken our fallen nature, He showed what it might become."—*Ibid.,* bk. 3, p. 134. Many times Ellen White refers to the *fallen* nature of Christ, the *fallen* condition, the *sinful* nature. See *Early Writings,* p. 150; Letter 106, 1896; *Medical Ministry,* p. 181; Manuscript 94, 1893; *Review and Herald* February 24, 1874 and December 15, 1896; *S.D.A. Bible Commentary,* vol. 5, p. 1131; *Selected Messages,* bk. 1, p. 253; *The Story of Redemption,* p. 44. She does not imply that this is imputed to Him; she says that this is His by experience. "The nature of God, whose law had been transgressed, and the nature of Adam, the transgressor, meet in Jesus, the Son of God, and the Son of man."—Manuscript 141, 1901. "It was in the order of God that Christ should take upon himself the form and nature of fallen man."—*Spiritual Gifts,* vol. 4a, p. 115. It was important that Christ take both the form and *nature* of fallen man.

If Christ did not fully descend to our level, Satan would have cried "foul" immediately, and nothing in the name of justice would have been accomplished in answering basic questions in the plan of salvation. To place Him above our nature, living in Adam's nature, is to obscure the amazing victory He gained for us.

"Though He had all the strength of passion of humanity, never did He yield to temptation to do one single act which was not pure and elevating and ennobling."—*In*

Heavenly Places, p. 155. He experienced the strength of our passion. He knew our weaknesses. He knew our attitudes. He knew our feelings. "Adam was tempted by the enemy, and he fell. It was not indwelling sin which caused him to yield; for God made him pure and upright, in His own image. He was as faultless as the angels before the throne. There was in him no corrupt principles, no tendencies to evil. But when Christ came to meet the temptations of Satan, He bore 'the likeness of sinful flesh.' "—*Signs of the Times*, October 17, 1900. When Jesus Christ bore the likeness of sinful flesh, it was not the nature of Adam, who was as faultless as the angels before the throne, without any tendencies to evil within him. But Jesus bore the likeness of sinful flesh. "He knows by experience what are the weaknesses of humanity, what are our wants, and where lies the strength of our temptations; for He was 'in all points tempted like as we are, yet without sin.' "—*The Ministry of Healing*, p. 71.

Where does the strength of our temptations lie? Surely within our inward nature which has a bent to evil. He knows *by experience* what that is. "Christ did in reality unite the offending nature of man with his own sinless nature."—*Review and Herald*, July 17, 1900. Notice that He united the *offending* nature of man with His sinless nature. Adam's nature before the fall was *not* an offending nature. It was a pure nature; it was a beautiful nature. A nature which automatically wants to do right is not an offending nature. It seems clear that we have excellent evidence from the Bible and the spirit of prophecy to say that Jesus Christ was born as we are born, with the tendencies and the attitudes that we receive.

No Sinful Propensities

But there is another aspect to our Lord's humanity. Jesus wasn't exactly the same as we are, because He had a Father who was the Holy Spirit.

Ellen White pens some important cautions. "Be careful, exceedingly careful as to how you dwell upon the human nature of Christ. Do not set Him before the people as a man with the propensities of sin. He is the second Adam. The first Adam was created a pure, sinless being, without a taint of sin upon him; he was the image of God. . . . Because of sin his posterity was born with inherent propensities of disobedience. But Jesus Christ was the only begotten Son of God. He took upon Himself human nature, and was tempted in all points as human nature is tempted. He could have sinned; He could have fallen, but not for one moment was there in Him an evil propensity. He was assailed with temptations in the wilderness, as Adam was assailed with temptations in Eden.

"Never, in any way, leave the slightest impression upon human minds that a taint of, or inclination to, corruption rested upon Christ. . . . Let every human being be warned from the ground of making Christ altogether human, such an one as ourselves; for it cannot be."—Ellen G. White comments, *S.D.A. Bible Commentary*, vol. 5, pp. 1128, 1129. "He is a brother in our infirmities, but not in possessing like passions. As the sinless One, His nature recoiled from evil. He endured struggles and torture of soul in a world of sin."—*Testimonies*, vol. 2, p. 202. "He was a mighty petitioner, not possessing the passions of our human, fallen natures, but compassed with like infirmities."—*Ibid.*, p. 509.

Now we must begin by examining Ellen White's use of the word *"propensity."* The evidence indicates that she used the word with different shades of meaning in different contexts. Sometimes *propensity* may refer to natural human tendencies, such as unfallen Adam had, while in other cases it may refer to fallen human tendencies. But when Ellen White qualifies the word *propensity* with adjectives such as evil, sinful, selfish, or worldly, the meaning is ever clearer.

For instance, she says, "We need not retain one sinful propensity."—Ellen G. White comments, *S.D.A. Bible Commentary,* vol. 7, p. 943. If *propensity* here means what we inherit, this statement could not be true, because we will retain our inherited nature until the day of death or translation. But if *propensity* refers to chosen or cultivated habit patterns, then it is true that we need not retain one of these sinful propensities. "Self-indulgence, self-pleasing, pride, and extravagance must be renounced. We cannot be Christians and gratify these propensities."—*Review and Herald,* May 16, 1893. These propensities are clearly chosen patterns of thought. We might even say that a sinful propensity refers to a cultivated tendency. The crucial point is that a sinful propensity is permitted to *develop* from our inherited bent to evil. Jesus never developed such sinful propensities.

Ellen White also uses the word *passion* in different ways. In some cases *passion* refers to acceptable human desires passed on by natural heredity. Thus she can say that Jesus accepted "all the strength of passion of humanity." She also uses *passion* in a more negative sense, referring to the development of the sinful tendencies passed on through the inherited stream. Jesus did not possess such passions. Once again the crucial distinction is between that which is inherited by birth, for which we are not guilty and for which Christ was not guilty, and the sinful propensities and passions which sinners choose to develop after birth, but which Christ never developed.

Many have wondered why we develop these propensities while Christ did not develop them. It must be admitted that this is the period of Christ's life (from birth to the age of accountability) about which we have very little information in the inspired writings. Therefore any conclusions must remain somewhat tentative. One suggestion is that the parents of Jesus took special care to guide the developing mind of the infant Jesus so that sinful propensities did not develop in Jesus. Another suggestion is that the ability to discern between right and wrong was present very early in the child Jesus and was exercised to prevent sinful propensities from developing. Another suggestion is that Christ was not intended to be an example to mankind as an infant; therefore events during His infancy are not relevant to issues in the great controversy. The solution that I favor is that because of the supernatural birth of Christ through the Holy Spirit, He was born much as we are reborn. Because the power of the Holy Spirit was directing His life from birth, He did not develop the sinful habit patterns or propensities which we develop from birth.

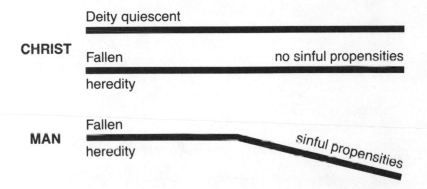

No matter which solution is adopted for the early years of Jesus' life, the central issue must not be obscured. If Jesus' life is to have any meaning as an *example* for us, then it is crucial that He inherit just what I inherit. No matter what choices I make, I cannot change my fallen nature. I cannot have the nature of prefall Adam, no matter how fully I surrender to God. If Jesus' perfect obedience was predicated upon the fact that He had an unfallen nature, then He had an advantage I can never possess. However, if Jesus' obedience was based on the Holy Spirit's control of His life, then I can also choose that control for my life, and I can come to live a life of total obedience. I can have that "advantage."

The following statement may be a good summary of this point. "Christ did not possess the same sinful, corrupt, fallen disloyalty we possess, for then He could not be a perfect offering."—Manuscript, 94, 1893. It is the disloyalty that is the problem. Inheritance does not make us guilty, but the choice to exercise our fallen nature produces guilt. Ellen White draws these points together in one decisive sentence. "In taking upon Himself man's nature in its fallen condition, Christ did not in the least participate in its sin. . . . We should have no misgivings in regard to the perfect sinlessness of the human nature of Christ."—*Selected Messages,* bk. 1, p. 256. Jesus took man's nature in its fallen condition, but He never participated in sin. He did not choose in the way we choose. Jesus was the spotless Lamb of God in a fallen body and nature.

Harry Johnson, referring to the inheritance that Jesus received, says, "Christ must have stooped to the level of fallen man, and accepted the voluntary humiliation of descending to the level to which man had fallen through the sin of Adam and through the sins of succeeding generations. . . . Mankind was not in the state of Adam before the Fall, and so the usual answer that Christ assumed perfect human nature, human nature as God originally created it, has the effect of weakening the force of the parallel. Man was not in the state of Adam before the Fall, and, as this was so, something far more drastic was needed if the effects of Adam's fall were to be overcome. If there was to come 'a second Adam to the fight,' then He must descend to the depths to which mankind had fallen . . . and in His own person lift mankind from its fallen depths to a new level of life." Jesus Christ had to come down to the level at which He found man after the Fall, not just to the level at which He originally created man.

Johnson continues, "If Jesus assumed perfect human nature untouched by the Fall, then it would mean that He did not stand side by side with man in his need. . . . If Jesus had assumed 'unfallen human nature' there would have been a gulf between Jesus and those whom He represented before God, the gulf created by sin. . . . He stood at the side of sinners in that He had assumed a human nature affected by the Fall. . . . If Jesus assumed perfect human nature, He spanned the gulf between God and man, but that between fallen and unfallen man still needed to be bridged. If, however, Christ shared our 'fallen human nature,' then His mediatorial work as High Priest bridges the whole gulf from fallen man in his dire need to God. It is for reasons of soteriology that this hypothesis about the Person of Christ is needed." (Harry Johnson, *The Humanity of the Saviour*, London, The Epworth Press, 1962, pp. 87, 124, 125)

What Was Satan's Charge?

It has been said that the accusation made by Satan against God was that unfallen man, Adam, could not obey the law of God. Therefore Jesus had to take Adam's nature to prove that Satan's charge was wrong. Some claim that Satan's charge had nothing to do with fallen man, but had only to do with perfect man. They maintain that Satan charged that perfect man could not obey the law of God.

However, the following clear statements tell us that exactly the opposite is true. "Satan, the fallen angel, had declared that no man could keep the law of God after the disobedience of Adam. He claimed the whole race under his control."—*Selected Messages*, bk. 3, p. 136. "Satan declared that it was impossible for the sons and daughters of Adam to keep the law of God, and thus charged upon God a lack of wisdom and love. If they could not keep the law, then there was fault with the Lawgiver."—*Signs of the Times*, January 16, 1896. Who was he focusing his charge upon? Fallen man—the son and daughters of Adam. If *they* could not keep the law, then God's law was faulty. The charge was made in regard to our ability to keep the law. Ellen White continues: "Men who are under the control of Satan repeat these accusations against God, in asserting that men can not keep the law of God. Jesus humbled himself, clothing his divinity with humanity, in order that he might stand as the head and representative of the human family, and by both precept and example condemn sin in the flesh, and give the lie to Satan's charges." If Satan's charges were that *fallen* man could not obey the law of God, then the only way Jesus could give the lie to Satan's charges was by proving that *fallen* man could obey the law of God.

"Christ kept the law, proving beyond controversy that man also can keep it."—*Review and Herald*, May 7, 1901.

"He came to this world to be tempted in all points as we are, to prove to the universe that in this world of sin human beings can live lives that God will approve.

"Satan declared that human beings could not live without sin."—*Ibid.*, March 9, 1905. Where are the human beings that Satan says are not able to live without sin? They are in this world of sin. So Satan's charge is against *fallen* man, that he cannot obey the law of God. Satan is saying that we who are living today cannot obey the law of God. Thus Jesus Christ had to demonstrate that fallen man can obey the law. Satan's charge *and* Christ's answer involve *fallen* nature. If Satan's charge was not only against Adam but against us, then Christ's taking unfallen nature would not have met Satan's charge at all. Christ *had* to take fallen nature to meet Satan's charge.

How Was Jesus Tempted?

Hebrews 4:15 tells us that Jesus was tempted in all points like as we are, yet without sin. Being tempted in all points as we are means that He was tempted in the ways in which we are tempted. "If we had to bear anything which Jesus did not endure, then upon this point Satan would represent the power of God as insufficient for us. . . . He endured every trial to which we are subject."—*The Desire of Ages*, p. 24. "The enticements which Christ resisted were those that we find it so difficult to withstand."—*Ibid.*, p. 116. Are not our problems basically self and pride and the desires that come from our fallen natures? Do we not fall most often because of the inner desires that lead us astray? If Jesus did not have any of these, could it really be true that He was tempted in all points as we are?

"Christ was put to the closest test, requiring the strength of all His faculties to resist the inclination when in danger, to use His power to deliver Himself from peril."—Ellen G. White Comments, *S.D.A. Bible Commentary*, vol. 7, p. 930. Note that He had to resist the inclination to use His power. Where did that inclination come from if not from within, from His own desires? Why did Jesus say, "I seek not mine own will" (John 5:30), and "I came down from heaven, not to do mine own will" (John 6:38)? Why would it be necessary to say this if His own will was faultless and pure and holy? But if His own will and His own inclination were tending toward the negative, then it would make sense for Him to ask that His Father's will be done. "The human will of Christ would not have led him to the wilderness of temptation, to fast, and to be tempted of the devil. It would not have led him to endure humiliation, scorn, reproach, suffering, and death. His human nature shrank from all these things as decidedly as ours shrinks from them. . . . What did Christ live to do? It was the will of his heavenly Father."—*Signs of the Times,* October 29, 1894.

"We are too much in the habit of thinking that the Son of God was a being so entirely exalted above us that it is an impossibility for him to enter into our trials and temptations, and that he can have no sympathy with us in our weakness and frailties. This is because we do not take in the fact of his oneness with humanity. He took upon him the likeness of sinful flesh, and was made in all points like unto his brethren."—*Ibid.,* May 16, 1895. If He was truly coming to enter into our weakness and our temptations, then it must be true that He took all that makes us the way we are, so He can show us the way to overcome those weaknesses and temptations. "If He did not have man's nature, He could not be our example. If He was not a partaker of our nature, He could not have been tempted as man has been. If it were not possible for Him to yield to temptation, He could not be our helper."—*Selected Messages*, bk. 1, p. 408. In other words, He must live at our level. He must live the way we live. Jesus Christ our Saviour experienced our feelings. He experienced our temptations. He knew what it was like to want to go wrong. He knew what it was like to feel the temptation to rebel against God, and that temptation arose from within His nature. Jesus had to meet the battle as we do. He must "fight the battle as every child of humanity must fight it, at the risk of failure and eternal loss."—*The Desire of Ages*, p. 49.

How Did Jesus Overcome?

Jesus overcame by dependence upon His Father's power, through communion with His Father. "His divinity was hidden. He overcame in human nature, relying upon God for power."—*Youth's Instructor*, April 25, 1901. "With the same facilities that man may obtain, [He] withstood the temptations of Satan as man must withstand them."—*Selected Messages*, bk. 1, p. 252. "He exercised in His own behalf no power that is not freely offered to us. As man, He met temptation, and overcame in the strength given Him from God."—*The Desire of Ages*, p. 24.

Remember that the power of Adam's sinless nature is not offered to us. That would be a tremendous power in the battle against sin. For Adam it was natural to do right. For us it is natural to do wrong. The impulses are totally different. If the power of Adam's nature had been exercised by Jesus, that would have been a mighty power not freely offered to us. "If Christ had a special power which it is not the privilege of man to have, Satan would have made capital of this matter."—*Selected Messages*, bk. 3, p. 139.

Jesus' victory was remarkable, not because as God He acted like God, but because as man He did not act like every other man. Jesus in man's nature lived a life that Satan said could not be lived. The amazing aspect about Jesus' life was that He lived a life that was supposed to be impossible to live. If Jesus had lived a sinless life on any level other than our fallen level, the question "What does that prove?" would never have been answered.

"In our conclusions, we make many mistakes because of our erroneous views of the human nature of our Lord. When we give to His human nature a power that is not possible for man to have in his conflicts with Satan, we destroy the completeness of His humanity."—Ellen G. White Comments, *S.D.A. Bible Commentary*, vol. 7, p. 929. We simply do not have the power of Adam's nature available to us. The warning is clear that by giving to Jesus' human nature a power that we cannot have, we destroy the completeness of His humanity. "The Lord now demands that every son and daughter of Adam . . . serve Him in human nature which we now have. . . . Jesus . . . could only keep the commandments of God in the same way that humanity can keep them."—*Ibid*. How can we keep them? Certainly not in Adam's nature. We can only keep them in that nature which we now have—fallen nature. And Jesus kept the commandments of God in the same way that we are to keep them. Jesus overcame as we are to overcome.

Jesus' victory was the victory of dependence upon His Father. He overcame through daily surrender and prayer. See *Desire of Ages*, pp. 130, 756. "He was wholly dependent upon God, and in the secret place of prayer He sought divine strength, that He might go forth braced for duty and trial.

"As a man He supplicated the throne of God till His humanity was charged with a heavenly current that should connect humanity with divinity. Through continual communion He received life from God, that He might impart life to the world. His experience is to be ours."— *Ibid.*, p. 363.

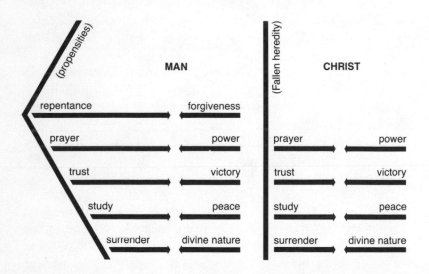

When Jesus came down to this earth, He accepted human nature with all its liabilities, but He was daily controlled by the Holy Spirit. He was filled with power from above that directed every step of His life and every act and every word. He lived His life totally in harmony with the will of God.

Obviously this understanding of the nature of Christ has definite implications for us. "We also are to overcome as Christ overcame."—*Ibid.*, p. 389. "In his humanity, he laid hold of the divinity of God; and this every member of the human family has the privilege of doing. Christ did nothing, that human nature may not do if it partakes of the divine nature."—*Signs of the Times,* June 17, 1897. Every member of the human family can partake of the divinity of God just as Christ did. He didn't do something we can't do. "Jesus revealed no qualities, and exercised no powers, that men may not have through faith in Him. His perfect humanity is that which all His followers may possess, if they will be in subjection to God as He was."—*The Desire of Ages,* p. 664. "The obedience of Christ to His Father was the same obedience that is required of man. . . . He came not to our world to give the obedience of a lesser God to a greater, but as a man to obey God's holy law, and in this way He is our example. The Lord Jesus came to our world, not to reveal what a God could do, but what a man could to, through faith in God's power to help in every emergency."—Ellen G. White Comments, *S.D.A. Bible Commentary,* vol. 7, p. 929.

"Christ came to live the law in His human character in just that way in which all may live the law in human nature if they will do as Christ was doing.

"Abundant provision has been made that finite, fallen man may so connect with God that, through the same Source by which Christ overcame in His human nature, he may stand firmly against every temptation, as did Christ."—*Selected Messages,* bk. 3, p. 130. Christ "laid hold on the throne of God, and there is not a man or woman who may not have access to the same help through faith in God. Man may become a partaker of the divine nature." "Divinity and humanity may be combined in them."—*Selected Messages,* bk. 1, p. 409. "It is the privilege of every believer in Christ to possess Christ's nature, a nature far above that which Adam forfeited by transgression."—*The Upward Look,* p. 180. "Christ . . . came to this earth to live the life of obedience God requires us to live."—(General Conference Bulletin, 1901, p. 481) "Just that which you may be He was in human nature."—Ellen G. White, Letter 106, 1896. "His life testified that by the aid of the same divine power which Christ received, it is possible for man to obey God's law."—*Selected Messages,* bk. 3, p. 132.

Our Saviour and Lord is both our Substitute and our Example. He gives both the assurance of forgiveness and the power to live above sin. He has demonstrated that we no longer need to live in rebellion. Jesus proved that with God the impossible is possible. The incarnation was God's greatest risk and His greatest victory in the cosmic controversy with Satan. Because of it our future is bright with hope.

Because of Christ's victory in our fallen nature, the way is now prepared for God to do the impossible in us, who share in the fallen nature of all humanity. What is totally impossible from a human perspective may simply be God's opportunity to accomplish the impossible once again.

Man's Impossibility— God's Possibility

Perfection seems to be a troublesome word these days. What does it really mean? What doesn't it mean? The first thing we should say is that perfection is the end result of righteousness by faith. It is not the method and it is not the foundation of righteousness by faith. It is the conclusion of the process of justification and sanctification.

Some believe that it is spiritually unhealthy to emphasize the subject of perfection. They suggest that to talk of sinlessness or perfection is dangerous because it takes glory away from Christ and robs Christians of their assurance of salvation, to the point that the coming of Jesus is dreaded rather than welcomed.

A student in one of my classes at Pacific Union College wrote a very clear summary of this attitude toward perfection. He suggested that perfection is impossible to define without defining sin, since perfection is the absence of sin. Since we are born into sin, our problem is the wrong desires we have inherited, which make it impossible for us to do anything but sin right up to the second coming of Christ. Even a fully surrendered Christian will think wrong thoughts suggested by his environment because of his sinful nature, and this will make him less

65

than perfect. He stated that Christ's sinless life was produced by His sinless nature. Christ is not our example
because He did not start on our level, and thus we cannot
be expected to finish on His level. The conclusion of this
student's paper was that perfection will be possible only
when our sinful nature is changed at the second coming.
Since we are sinful by nature, we cannot stop sinning in
this life.

Do you see how decisions about the nature of sin and
the nature of Christ will affect decisions in all areas of
righteousness by faith? If the ideas I have just summa-
rized are true, then we must redefine much of what we
have believed and taught for many years in the Seventh-
day Adventist Church. If these ideas are not true, then we
need to know why they are not. We need to take another
look at the evidence.

Definitions

It is crucial that we define *sin* and *sinlessness* and *perfection* as carefully as possible. If the primary meaning of
sin is sinful nature, then we become sinners when we are
born into this world. However, if the primary meaning of
sin is sinful character, then we become sinners because of
the choices that we make after we are able to choose between right and wrong. If *sin* is our nature, then we have
no control over that, and we are sinners by nature. If *sin*
is our character, then we do have control over the choices
we make, and we are sinners by choice.

On the same basis, if *sinlessness* means a sinless nature, then that is possible only at the second coming of
Christ, because we retain our sinful natures until that
time. However, if *sinlessness* means a sinless character,
then that is possible whenever we choose not to sin.
Our definition of sin is the determining factor. If we
mean nature when we use the word *sin,* then there can be
no sinlessness until the second coming of Christ. If we

mean character when we use the term *sin,* then sinlessness is a possibility before the second coming of Christ.

With these definitions in mind, let's analyze the word *perfection.* There are at least four definitions of *perfection* that are relevant here. The first is absolute perfection. Sometimes it is said that we as human beings can never be absolutely perfect. This is correct, for absolute perfection describes God Himself. There is no other absolute perfection. Thus, absolute perfection is never possible for created beings—not for human beings and not for angels. "Angelic perfection failed in heaven. Human perfection failed in Eden."—*Our High Calling,* p. 45.

When Lucifer first began to suggest that God was unjust, nearly half of the angelic host listened to him and thought that he might be right. See *The Story of Redemption,* p. 18. Then God held a heavenly council in which He set forth the truth about Jesus Christ being fully God, thus showing Lucifer's challenge to be unfounded. See *Patriarchs and Prophets,* p. 36. After that council, approximately one third of the angels sided with Lucifer and were cast out of heaven. (See *Testimonies,* vol. 3, p. 115.)

This means that a significant number of the angels who had listened to Lucifer and had thought he might be right changed their minds. Therefore, we cannot use the term absolute perfection to describe these angels who changed their minds about God and Lucifer. In fact, the angels were not fully convinced that God was right and Satan was wrong until the cross. Up to that point some of them apparently were not fully convinced that Satan's changes were false. Only then was Satan fully removed from their affections. Their sympathy for him ended at the cross. See *The Desire of Ages,* pp. 758-761. Surely then, it is fair to say that absolute perfection is not a term we can apply in discussing righteousness by faith, since it does not even apply to angels, but only to God.

The second definition of *perfection* is nature perfection. Our sinful nature will be removed only at the second coming of Christ, after which there will be no more sinful promptings from within. Thus, nature perfection, which involves removal of temptation from within, will occur only at the second coming of Christ. We cannot experience nature perfection before then.

However, if our definitions of *sin* and *sinlessness* focus on character, then we can discuss meanings of *perfection* that are possible for us today. There are at least two aspects of character which can be described by the words *perfect,* or *perfection.* The first is character surrender. This occurs at the moment of conversion, when we surrender our lives completely to Christ. At that moment we are accounted perfect in Christ. Our perfection is complete at that time, but we're just beginning the walk of Christ. We are fully surrendered to the degree that we understand ourselves and God's will for us. God will accept the full surrender of all that we know about ourselves at that time. Thus our character surrender is perfect, because it is counted as perfect by God.

But there is another concept that we must examine—character maturity. If we believe that sin is on the basis of choice, then we must also believe that we can choose not to sin. Character maturity is simply the ripening of the harvest in the individual life. We are becoming mature in Christ when we are no longer choosing to sin against God. We choose not to rebel, and that choice can occur at any time. If Jesus Christ does live within us through the processes of justification and sanctification, then when He controls our lives, we do not sin because Christ does not sin. Christ does nothing that is out of harmony with His will. When we sin, we are choosing

Satan's control. We are choosing to let Satan operate in our lives.

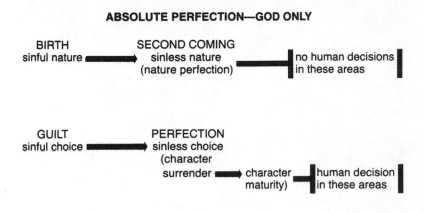

ABSOLUTE PERFECTION—GOD ONLY

BIRTH
sinful nature ➡ SECOND COMING
sinless nature
(nature perfection) ➡ no human decisions
in these areas

GUILT
sinful choice ➡ PERFECTION
sinless choice
(character
surrender ➡ character
maturity) ➡ human decision
in these areas

This concept can be expressed in a simple but clear way. Christ in—sin out. Sin in—Christ out. We cannot have Christ and sin reigning on the throne of the life at the same time. Christ will not accept a divided heart. In a mature character Christ is controlling totally, and therefore we are not making rebellious choices. We are choosing not to rebel against God in thought, in word, or in action. What we are doing here is focusing on what God can do, not on what I can't do. We can talk for hours about the impossibilities of fallen man, but why not speak of the possibilities of God? Why can't we talk about what is possible?

In regard to our definitions, the definitions that are most important for our study are those categories over which we exercise control. If we believe that sin is by choice, then we will also believe that we can choose to obey. We can choose to surrender, and we can choose to grow into maturity. Because Christ provides the power for victory, a sinless character is possible for all surrendered Christians. Thus, perfection, carefully defined, is a reality. It is not an impossibility. It is the areas over which we exercise control that we must study.

The new birth brings perfection in Christ, which is always sufficient for salvation. We are saved on the basis of that surrender. The problem is that we interrupt our surrender to Christ. The power of Christ who dwells in us does not change, but our surrender to Christ is not constant. It is the interruptions that can and should cease, for we should let Christ control us totally at all times. The variable factor is the constancy of our surrender. The power of Christ is constant, but our relationship wavers at times.

By nature we will always be sinful until Christ comes. But we can decide to make no choices against God's will. We can actually have a sinless character in a sinful nature. Here we see the vital importance of a correct understanding of Christ's nature. If Christ overcame the promptings of His sinful nature by the Holy Spirit's control, then the same method is available to us. However, if Christ did not have our nature, then the method is unclear. It is important to be reminded at this point that guilt is not imputed because of our nature, but only because of choices made and character developed.

Perfection in the Bible

Jude 24 expresses a very important truth about what Christ can do. "Now unto him that is able to keep you from falling, and to present you faultless before the presence of his glory with exceeding joy." Is Christ able to keep us from falling? Jude under inspiration says He is able to keep us from falling. Thus, falling is not an inevitable reality of our lives. Christ is able to keep us from falling. In Philippians 4:13 we find another statement that we must look at seriously. "I can do all things through Christ which strengtheneth me." Are *all* things possible through Jesus Christ? Is it really true that victory over sin is possible?

Second Peter 2:9 says, "The Lord knoweth how to deliver the godly out of temptations." Then it is not necessary for us to yield to temptation, because He can deliver us from temptation. We cannot deliver ourselves from temptation, but God can. He will provide a way of escape if we're willing. First Corinthians 10:13 adds, "There hath no temptation taken you but such as is common to man: but God is faithful, who will not suffer you to be tempted above that ye are able; but will with the temptation also make a way to escape, that ye may be able to bear it." God has promised that He will not let any temptation come to us that is too strong for us, which would make our fall inevitable. This means that a way of escape is available for every temptation. There is not one temptation that comes to us that makes sin inevitable. God has promised that if we will trust in Him, He will show us the way out of every temptation.

First Peter 2:21, 22 states, "For even hereunto were ye called: because Christ also suffered for us, leaving us an example, that ye should follow his steps: who did no sin, neither was guile found in his mouth." We know that Christ lived a life without sin, but sometimes we don't want to recognize the fact that He is also our example, bidding us to follow in His steps. Of course, this assumes that Christ was born the way we are born, feeling our temptations and experiencing our desires. If all that was true for Him and He did not sin, then He can be an example for us.

First John 3:2-9 is a significant passage relating to our position after conversion. "Beloved, now are we the sons of God, and it doth not yet appear what we shall be: but we know that, when he shall appear, we shall be like him; for we shall see him as he is. And every man that hath this hope in him purifieth himself, even as he is pure. Whosoever committeth sin transgresseth also the law: for sin is the transgression of the law. And ye know that he was manifested to take away our sins; and in him is no sin. Whosoever abideth in him sinneth not: whosoever sinneth hath not seen him, neither known him. . . . He that committeth sin is of the devil; for the devil sinneth from the beginning. . . . Whosoever is born of God doth not commit sin; for his seed remaineth in him; and he cannot sin, because he is born of God." If we are in Christ, we are not rebelling against Him, and sin is rebellion. If we abide in Him, we will not sin, because He does not sin in us. Here we come back to our earlier statement that Christ does not sin. So if we are abiding in Christ constantly, He will not be sinning in us. Thus we will not be rebelling in thought or in word or in action as long as we are abiding in Him.

We find a magnificent statement in Revelation 3:21. "To him that overcometh will I grant to sit with me in my throne, even as I also overcame, and am set down with my Father in his throne." The model of overcoming is Jesus Christ, and we are to overcome even as He overcame. Certainly we must depend on His strength and power, but it remains true that we will overcome as He overcame. Second Corinthians 10:5 is another classic statement. "Casting down imaginations, and every high thing that exalteth itself against the knowledge of God, and bringing into captivity every thought to the obedience of Christ."

God's ideal for us is that we bring every thought into captivity to Christ. Not just the positive thoughts, but even the negative thoughts, so that He controls all of our thoughts and all our attitudes. Galatians 5:16 adds, "This I say then, Walk in the Spirit, and ye shall not fulfil the lust of the flesh." If the Holy Spirit is controlling, we will not succumb to the desires of our natures. We need not fall and fail constantly, over and over again. The promise of Scripture is that we can overcome and that we can gain continual victories in the battle against the flesh.

Perfection in the Spirit of Prophecy

Ellen White speaks clearly and powerfully on the subject of growth to maturity. "We can overcome. Yes; fully, entirely. Jesus died to make a way of escape for us, that we might overcome every evil temper, every sin, every temptation, and sit down at last with Him."—*Testimonies,* vol. 1, p. 144. Please note that every sin is to be overcome. But we should remember as we read these statements that we overcome, not by our own strength, but only through surrender to the power of God, as we allow Jesus to dwell within us constantly. "If you will stand under the bloodstained banner of Prince Emmanuel, faithfully doing His service, you need never yield to temptation; for One stands by your side who is able to keep you from falling."—*Our High Calling,* p. 19. What a marvelous statement. We need never yield to *any* temptation. Why? Because One stands by our side who is able to keep us from falling. The power of God is stronger than the power of Satan. If we keep Him on the throne of the heart constantly, we need never fall.

"There is no excuse for sinning. A holy temper, a Christlike life, is accessible to every repenting, believing child of God."—*The Desire of Ages,* p. 311. But let us look back to the immediate context of this statement. Ellen White speaks about God's ideal for His children being higher than the highest human thought can reach and refers to Jesus' command to be perfect as the Father in heaven is perfect. She says that this command is a promise and that God wants us to be completely free from the power of Satan.

"The tempter's agency is not to be accounted an excuse for one wrong act. Satan is jubilant when he hears the professed followers of Christ making excuses for their deformity of character. It is these excuses that lead to sin." In light of these thoughts, Ellen White says that there is no excuse for sinning. Are we not in danger of making excuses when we say, "I sin every day. I cannot help but sin. It is my nature to sin. Sinning is inevitable"? Do we not make Satan jubilant when we make excuses for our deformed characters? There is no excuse for sinning. We certainly have an excuse for being born in a sinful world and inheriting a fallen nature, because we have no choice or control over that, but we do have a choice and we do have control over sinning. This is what Ellen White means when she refers to perfection and sinlessness.

Ellen White tells us that if we will be in subjection to God as Christ was, we may possess His perfect humanity. See *The Desire of Ages,* p. 664. "Not even by a thought did He yield to temptation. So it may be with us."—*The Desire of Ages,* p. 123. It is really an amazing concept that we need not yield to temptation even by a thought if we are being controlled by Jesus. "The life that Christ lived in this world, men and women can live through His power and under His instruction. In their conflict with Satan they may have all the help that He had. They may be more than conquerors through Him who loved them and gave Himself for them."—*Testimonies,* vol. 9, p. 22. We've already seen that Christ had nothing available to Him which we do not have. His power came from the Holy Spirit's control of His life, and we can have that same power if we submit to God as He did. (More detail is given in the chapter "How Did Christ Live?")

Christ came to this earth to show us that we can obey God's law if we depend on the power of God as He did. See *Review and Herald,* July 4, 1912. "That life in you will produce the same character and manifest the same works as it did in Him. Thus you will be in harmony with every precept of His law."—*Thoughts From the Mount of Blessings,* p. 78. These statements make it clear that (1) God's law can be obeyed, and (2) obedience is possible only through the dynamic power of God permeating and controlling the weak, sinful nature which is ours by inheritance.

The following statement points up one of the purposes of the incarnation. Christ came with our weak, fallen nature to show us that we need not be discouraged because we have inherited a fallen nature. He proved for our encouragement that if humanity is controlled by divinity there is no need for sin in the life. "The Saviour took upon Himself the infirmities of humanity and lived a sinless life, that men might have no fear that because of the weakness of human nature they could not overcome. Christ came to make us 'partakers of the divine nature,' and His life declares that humanity, combined with divinity, does not commit sin."—*The Ministry of Healing,* p. 180. "Christ came to this earth and lived a life of perfect obedience, that men and women, through his grace, might also live lives of perfect obedience. This is necessary to their salvation."—*Review and Herald,* March 15, 1906. Whatever Christ did, including His perfect obedience, is open to all who will use the same method of overcoming that He used.

Ellen White is very explicit in stating that the cause for our failures and sins lies in our own will rather than in our weakened human nature. (See *Christ's Object Lessons,* p. 331.) "Through the plan of redemption, God has provided means for subduing every sinful trait, and resisting every temptation, however strong."—*Selected Messages,* bk. 1, p. 82. It is a recurring concept in her writings that every temptation can be resisted by the power of Christ. If, indeed, every temptation is turned away by the will, then the result will inevitably be that we will not be sinning.

The concept of living without sinning is precisely the focus of the following three statements. The power of an abiding Christ is stronger than any temptation to sin. "Do not settle down in Satan's easy chair, and say that there is no use, you cannot cease to sin, that there is no power in you to overcome. There is no power in you apart from Christ, but it is your privilege to have Christ abiding in your heart by faith, and He can overcome sin in you, when you cooperate with His efforts."—*Our High Calling,* p. 76. "To every one who surrenders fully to God is given the privilege of living without sin, in obedience to the law of heaven." "God requires of us perfect obedience."—*Review and Herald,* September 27, 1906. "Christ died to make it possible for you to cease to sin, and sin is the transgression of the law."—*Review and Herald,* August 28, 1894.

Ellen White stresses that God requires moral perfection. We must never lower the standard because of inherited or cultivated tendencies toward sin. In fact, imperfection of character is sin and must be corrected. As the individual moves toward a perfect character this manifests itself in "perfection in action." See *Christ's Object Lessons,* pp. 330-332. Some have tried to make a separation between one's relationship with God and one's behavior, claiming that one can have a living relationship with God even though one's behavior might be quite faulty. It should be crystal clear that when the motivation and desires of the heart are in harmony with God's will, the outward actions will follow suit.

When writing about the last events in this earth's history, Ellen White is very specific that God's people will be gaining victories over personal sins. "But before that time shall come [the second coming], everything that is imperfect in us will have been seen and put away. All envy and jealousy and evil surmising and every selfish plan will have been banished from the life."—*Selected*

Messages, bk. 3, p. 427. This statement proves conclusively that God's people will *not* be sinning right up to the second coming of Christ, as some claim. Even sinful motives and feelings will be overcome by the power of Christ *before* the second coming.

We now have come to an extremely important principle in our consideration of the subject of perfection. Why is perfection important? What does it prove? "The very image of God is to be reproduced in humanity. The honor of God, the honor of Christ, is involved in the perfection of the character of His people."—*The Desire of Ages,* p. 671. "The honor of Christ must stand complete in the perfection of the character of his chosen people."—*Signs of the Times,* November 25, 1897. The purpose of character perfection is not so that we can be saved. Salvation has already been accomplished by character surrender at the time of justification. Perfection has to do with the credibility of God's word. God has said that His law is reasonable and can be obeyed. Satan has challenged this claim, and the final decision has not been rendered.

God's remnant people will have a role to play in the vindication of the credibility of His word. In fact, God will vindicate His own name by providing His people with the divine power necessary to obey His law perfectly. "If there ever was a people in need of constantly increasing light from heaven, it is the people that, in this time of peril, God has called to be the depositaries of His holy law and to vindicate His character before the world."—*Testimonies,* vol. 5, p. 746. "How is the world to be enlightened, save by the lives of Christ's followers?" "God's people are to reflect to the world the bright rays of his glory." "God has plainly stated that he expects us to be perfect, and because he expects this, he has made provision for us to be partakers of the divine nature."—*Review and Herald,* January 28, 1904. Thus the perfect character developed by God's people is crucially important to the final resolution of the great controversy between Christ and Satan. In fact, this reason for stressing the concept of perfection in God's end-time people may well be the issue in a nutshell. God's claim is that total obedience is possible. Satan's claim is that a sinful nature and character makes obedience impossible. Who is telling the truth? Only God's remnant can prove Satan to be liar.

It will be totally impossible for any of us to receive the seal of God while we have defective characters. There can be no stain or defilement on our soul temples. (See *Testimonies,* vol. 5, p. 214.) "Now, while our great High Priest is making the atonement for us, we should seek to become perfect in Christ. Not even by a thought could our Saviour be brought to yield to the power of temptation. . . . Satan could find nothing in the Son of God that would enable him to gain the victory. He had kept His Father's commandments, and there was no sin in Him that Satan could use to his advantage. This is the condition in which those must be found who shall stand in the time of trouble."—*The Great Controversy,* p. 623.

One important concept in our study of perfection is that perfection is never static. Perfection is not a plateau. "Jesus, considered as a man, was perfect, yet He grew in grace. . . . Even the most perfect Christian may increase continually in the knowledge and love of God.

"Jesus sits as a refiner and purifier of His people; and when His image is perfectly reflected in them, they are perfect and holy, and prepared for translation. A great work is required of the Christian. We are exhorted to cleanse ourselves from all filthiness of the flesh and spirit, perfecting holiness in the fear of God."—*Testimonies,* vol. 1, pp. 339, 340.

Perfection is *growth*. Even when the mature Christian is no longer rebelling against God, there will be much to learn about God and oneself. Development will be a continuous process, even throughout eternity. When rebellion is eliminated from the life and the Christian no longer succumbs to the blandishments of Satan, character growth will be phenomenal as the Christian moves upward *in* perfection.

It is sometimes claimed that Ellen White never states that we will be sinless this side of the second coming. The following two statements are very clear about sinlessness occurring *prior* to the second coming. "Everyone who by faith obeys God's commandments will reach the condition of sinlessness in which Adam lived before his transgression."—*In Heavenly Places,* p. 146; see also *S.D.A. Commentary,* vol. 6, p. 1118. This remarkable statement says that we *will* reach the condition of sinlessness in which Adam lived before his transgression. Obviously this means that Ellen White is using a definition of sinlessness which has to do with character. She means that we can have a sinless character, not a sinless nature.

"Christ has made every provision for the sanctification of His Church. He has made abundant provision for every soul to have such grace and strength that he will be more than a conqueror in the warfare against sin. . . . He came to this world and lived a sinless life, that in His power His people might also live lives of sinlessness. He desires them by practicing the principles of truth to show to the world that God's grace has power to sanctify the heart."—*Review and Herald,* April 1, 1902. Notice that the context of this statement is sanctification and the ongoing battle against sin. In this time of preparation *before* the close of probation, during the process of sanctification, we can live sinless lives. Ellen White is clearly not afraid of saying that we can live sinless lives, just as Jesus lived a sinless life in this world. Once again this assumes a definition of sinlessness as a sinless character.

One thing is *not* changed at the second coming of

Christ—character. Our character traits, developed during this probationary time, will not be changed by the resurrection. We will have the same dispositions in heaven that we have developed on earth. Since character is not changed at the second coming, it is vitally important that character transformation occurs on a daily basis now. See *The Adventist Home,* p. 16.

Lest this high standard discourage any sincere Christian, we have the promise that whatever God expects of His children He provides by His grace. "Our Saviour does not require impossibilities of any soul. He expects nothing of His disciples that He is not willing to give them grace and strength to perform. He would not call upon them to be perfect if He had not at His command every perfection of grace to bestow on the ones upon whom He would confer so high and holy a privilege." "Our work is to strive to attain in our sphere of action the perfection that Christ in His life on earth attained in every phase of character. He is our example."—*God's Amazing Grace,* p. 230. Here we have clear counsel that we are to depend upon Christ to make us perfect. He is the One who will perfect us. We cannot perfect ourselves. We must look to Christ as our Example and follow the plan that He has outlined.

Some have wondered why discussion of the nature of Christ should occupy the time and energy of students of the Bible today. Perhaps these statements will show the importance of this subject. "God requires perfection of character from his children." "We may say that it is impossible for us to reach God's standard; but when Christ came as our substitute and surety, it was as a human being. . . . With his divinity veiled by humanity, he lived a life of perfect obedience to the law of God." "As Christ lived the law in humanity, so we may do if we will take hold of the strong for strength."—*Signs of the Times,* March 4, 1897.

Do you see how important it is to understand the nature Christ took and the method He used to obey? "None need fail of attaining, in his sphere, to perfection of Christian character. . . . God calls upon us to reach the standard of perfection and places before us the example of Christ's character. In His humanity, perfected by a life of constant resistance of evil, the Saviour showed that through cooperation with Divinity, human beings may in this life attain to perfection of character. This is God's assurance to us that we, too, may obtain complete victory."—*The Acts of the Apostles,* p. 531.

If Christ's nature was different from ours, or if He used a different method of overcoming sin from what we can use, surely it would seem beyond any reasonable possibility that we could ever do what He did. But because His nature was our nature and His method was our method, we have hope for complete victory in our own lives. He showed us how to make the impossible possible, through His power and encouraged by His example. "In His life and character He not only reveals the character of God, but the possibility of man."—*Selected Messages,* bk. 1, p. 349. "He came to fulfill all righteousness, and, as the head of humanity, to show man that he can do the same work, meeting every specification of the requirements of God. . . . Perfection of character is attainable by every one who strives for it."—*God's Amazing Grace,* p. 141.

Ellen White was very strong in her reproof of those who denied the possibility of living perfect lives. "Exact obedience is required, and those who say that it is not possible to live a perfect life throw upon God the imputation of injustice and untruth."—Manuscript 148, 1899. The reasons she insisted on the necessity of believing in the possibility of perfection were twofold: First, because of the psychological danger of excusing one's personal sins, and, second, the need to keep uppermost in mind the power of Christ to give victory over any and all personal sins. "To love and cherish sin, is to love and cherish its author, that deadly foe of Christ. When they [God's professed people] excuse sin and cling to perversity of character, they give Satan a place in their affections, and pay him homage."— *Our High Calling,* p. 321. "He who has not sufficient faith in Christ to believe that he can keep him from sinning, has not the faith that will give him an entrance into the kingdom of God."—*Review and Herald,* March 10, 1904.

These are typical Ellen White statements in the area of perfection and sinlessness. She is constantly talking about overcoming and claiming that we do not need to yield to temptation. She asserts that we can, through dependence upon the power of Christ, overcome as He overcame. He showed us how, and we can follow in His footsteps. Over and over again Ellen White says that we can live lives of obedience to God, and she is comfortable using the word *sinlessness* when she uses the term in this context.

The question many seem to be asking today is, Has anyone ever achieved this perfection of character? Who among us is perfect? Ellen White responds, "The godly character of this prophet [Enoch] represents the state of holiness which must be attained by those who shall be 'redeemed from the earth'. . . at the time of Christ's second advent."—*Patriarchs and Prophets,* pp. 88, 89. She describes Enoch as finding it necessary to live in a time when moral pollution was teeming all around him, but his mind was upon God and heavenly things. His face was lighted up with the light that shines in the face of Jesus. The atmosphere he breathed was tainted with sin and corruption, yet he lived a life of holiness and was unsullied with the prevailing sins of the age. See *Testimonies,* vol. 2, p. 122. Apparently Enoch chose not to sin. He chose to put his life in harmony with Christ's life at a time when things were as bad as they have ever been in this world's history.

"Some few in every generation from Adam resisted his every artifice and stood forth as noble representatives of what it was in the power of man to do and to be. . . . Enoch and Elijah are the correct representatives of what the race might be through faith in Jesus Christ if they chose to be. Satan was greatly disturbed because these noble, holy men stood untainted amid the moral pollution surrounding them, perfected righteous characters, and were accounted worthy for translation to Heaven. As they had stood forth in moral power in noble uprightness, overcoming Satan's temptations, he could not bring them under the dominion of death. He triumphed that he had power to overcome Moses with his temptations, and that he could mar his illustrious character and lead him to the sin of taking glory to himself before the people which belonged to God."—*The Review and Herald,* March 3, 1894.

Apparently there was something special about the characters developed by Enoch and Elijah before their translation. They did, in fact, choose to resist sin by the power of God. Then we find this beautiful statement, "And there are Enochs in this our day."—*Christ's Object Lessons,* p. 332. So has anyone achieved this type of perfection of character? The answer seems obvious.

Should We Claim to Be Perfect?

Ellen White's answer to this question is very clear. "The closer you come to Jesus, the more faulty you will appear in your own eyes; for your vision will be clearer, and your imperfections will be seen in broad and distinct contrast to His perfect nature. This is evidence that Satan's delusions have lost their power."—*Steps to Christ,* pp. 64, 65. The more our lives come into harmony with Jesus, the less we will see that is good in ourselves. The closer we come to His ideal, the more unworthy we will feel. "The nearer we come to Jesus, and the more clearly we discern the purity of His character, the more clearly shall we see the exceeding sinfulness of sin, and the less shall we feel like exalting ourselves."—*The Acts of the Apostles,* p. 561.

Then will we claim to be perfect or sinless? "Those who are really seeking to perfect Christian character will never indulge the thought that they are sinless."—*The Sanctified Life,* p. 7. "We shall not boast of our holiness. . . . We cannot say, 'I am sinless,' till this vile body is changed and fashioned like unto His glorious body."— *Signs of the Times,* March 23, 1888. "When the conflict of life is ended, . . . when the saints of God are glorified, then and then only will it be safe to claim that we are saved and sinless."—*Ibid.,* May 16, 1895.

These passages refer to the *claim* to sinlessness, to the thought in our minds that we are without sin. Please note that the last statement said that only when we are glorified will it be safe to claim that we are *saved* and sinless. Are we to be in a saved condition right now, in which we would be saved if we were to die? I believe the Bible assures us that we can be confident that we are saved in Christ right now. But Ellen White warns us that not until glorification will it be safe to *claim* that we are saved. So there is a difference between *being* saved and claiming that we are saved.

If this be true, could there be a difference between *being* sinless and *claiming* that we are sinless? "No one who claims holiness is really holy. Those who are registered as holy in the books of heaven are not aware of the fact, and are the last ones to boast of their own goodness."—*The Faith I Live By,* p. 140. Here we have clear evidence that those whom God calls holy will never claim to be holy, showing that there can be a difference between being sinless and claiming to be sinless.

Should we ever claim to be sinless? The claim to sinlessness will never be made by the one who is most in harmony with the will of God, because the closer we come to God, the less we will feel like claiming anything for ourselves. We will feel like casting all at the foot of the cross—our glory, our pride, and whatever we have accomplished. There well may be, even today, those who are so much in harmony with the will of God that they are not rebelling in thought, word, or action. But they will be the last ones to claim that condition.

The Close of Probation

If we really believe that there is a close of probation and that God is demonstrating something special after the close of probation, then it seems that we must also believe in full character maturity, which means living without yielding to sinful desires. After the close of probation, "there will be no Priest in the sanctuary to offer their sacrifices, their confessions, and their prayers before the Father's throne."—*Early Writings,* p. 48. "I also saw that many do not realize what they must be in order to live in the sight of the Lord without a high priest in the sanctuary through the time of trouble. Those who receive the seal of the living God and are protected in the time of trouble must reflect the image of Jesus fully." "There will be no time then to do it and no Mediator to plead their cause before the Father."—*Ibid,* p. 71. "Those who are living upon the earth when the intercession of Christ shall cease in the sanctuary above are to stand in the sight of a holy God without a mediator. Their robes must be spotless, their characters must be purified from sin by the blood of sprinkling. Through the grace of God and their own diligent effort they must be conquerors in the battle with evil."—*The Great Controversy,* p. 425.

There will be a difference in heaven after the close of probation, in that there will be no priestly ministry by Jesus. There will be no Intercessor, no Mediator, pleading the cause of sinners before the Father. Now this does not imply that the enabling power of Jesus dwelling within His people on earth will be removed. But the priestly ministry of forgiveness comes to an end at the close of probation. "In that fearful time the righteous must live in the sight of a holy God without an intercessor."—*Ibid.*, p. 614. "After the close of Jesus' mediation, the saints were living in the sight of a holy God without an intercessor."—*The Story of Redemption*, p. 403. The ending of Christ's work of intercession means that there will be no more forgiveness of sins after the close of probation. If the ministry of forgiving sins will have ceased, then it seems imperative that there be no sinning on the part of those who are sealed to God after the close of probation. We can only be forgiven if Jesus is interceding for us and forgiving our sins.

I believe that the primary reason for a short delay before Christ's coming during which there is no Mediator is to dramatize before the watching universe the reality of God's complete power over sin in the lives of those whose wills are totally and forever united to His own. Some of the very people who formerly betrayed their sacred trust by agreeing with Satan that it was impossible to obey God's law will finally demonstrate that there really is no excuse for sin. The close of probation will play an important part in the final demonstration that God is making before His universe: that, indeed, it is possible for fallen man to obey God's law, which is righteous and good and holy.

If we take seriously the biblical admonitions to overcome, the reality of the close of probation, and the challenge of the 144,000, then we must also take seriously the truth of living without sinning. However, we must remember when we are discussing perfection, we are talking about the goal—the end result. Our focus needs to be on justification and sanctification, because this is the method of receiving salvation. Jesus forgives us of our sins. He comes into our lives with power and victory. As we focus on justification and sanctification, the end result or goal will naturally follow. It will be the natural result of letting God do His full work in our hearts. As an athlete running in a footrace focuses on the next few yards while remembering the tape that is at the end of the race, so the Christian focuses on His relationship with Christ today while remembering that there is a goal at the end of the race.

Summary of Biblical Perfection

First, we must be very clear as to what perfection is *not*. If we are to understand what perfection is, we must stay completely away from those concepts which are in opposition to the biblical doctrine of perfection. I believe that most of the objections to the doctrine of perfection are based upon misconceptions of what it is. Perfection is never absolute, either now or after the coming of Christ. Perfection is never equality with Christ. Perfection does not mean a lack of weakness or freedom from temptation. Perfection does not mean freedom from illness or an absence of mental or physical mistakes. No one who is perfect will ever feel that he is perfect.

The term *perfectionism* has a negative connotation in many minds. Strictly speaking, there should be nothing negative about the word, for it simply describes a belief in perfection. But in many minds, *perfectionism* describes an extreme and distorted view of perfection. Perfectionism, in this negative sense, emphasizes an absolute point beyond which there can be no further development. This belief actually grows out of Greek philosophy rather than the Bible. This distorted perfectionism focuses on a quality in man which can exist independently of the presence of an abiding Christ.

We do not want to be involved in extremist perfectionism because it is a self-centered legalism which places self on the throne of the heart once again and removes

Christ from the control of the life. It endeavors to force obedience, so that one becomes obedient through one's striving. This distorted perfectionism is extremely dangerous, but so is the doctrine of imperfection, which allows the sinfulness and helplessness of man to overshadow what God promises to do for repentant sinners through the empowering presence of the Holy Spirit.

To doubt that perfection is a realistic goal is to doubt the living power to accomplish that which God has promised. Imperfection does not understand Jesus as man's complete Substitute *and* Example, who demonstrated that God's law of love could be kept and that man could indeed be an overcomer here and now. I believe that the biblical doctrine of perfection is different from both the extremes of perfectionism and imperfection.

Having stated what perfection is *not,* I think it is necessary to say what perfection *is.* Perfection means being in so close a relationship with Christ that the individual ceases to respond to external or internal promptings to sin. Perfection means entire cooperation with Christ. Perfection means continuous death to self and a denial of one's own independent will and inclination. Perfection is total rejection of egotism and pride. Perfection is a merger of man's will with Christ's so that the Holy Spirit is in full and final control. Perfection is an unbroken exercise of faith which keeps the soul pure from every stain of sin or disloyalty to God. Perfection refers to the dynamic, growing life-style of the person who reflects the life of Jesus, so that he no longer yields to rebel, sinful desires. Perfection is Christlikeness, combining a relationship with God such as Jesus had, with the qualities of character which He manifested. Perfection is living a mature life in the Spirit, full of the fruits of the Spirit and thus without sin. If perfection is understood correctly, we will see it in terms of character maturity, which means that we live in harmony with Christ's will. He dwells within us, and this dwelling of Christ within us will preclude rebel, sinful desires from gaining control. Christ will control what we alone cannot control.

Although this doctrine seems to be clear in the New Testament and in Ellen White's writings, the thought lingers with some that surely God does not expect sinlessness in His people this side of translation. Perhaps this misinterpretation of what God is trying to say to His people is not deliberate, and may not even be conscious. This error begins with a misunderstanding of what sin is and how Christ lived as a man, and it is perpetuated in misunderstandings of righteousness by faith. You see, if Jesus was only man's Substitute but not his Example, then the challenge to do what He did is immeasurably reduced. "He [Satan] is constantly seeking to deceive the followers of Christ with his fatal sophistry that it is impossible for them to overcome."—*The Great Controversy,* p. 489.

Rightly understood, righteousness by faith in God's power to keep man from falling is a compelling, dynamic, positive force in a person's life. Knowing well his own weakness when separated from the power of God, the man of faith now sees what can be accomplished in his life, and he finds his greatest joy in living the victorious life. Then the message of the Bible becomes exceedingly simple. "Jesus did it, and through dependence on God, I can too. I can live as He did through faith in my heavenly Father." In this experience we will be living without rebel thoughts in any area of the life. We will have reached perfection of character in a fallen nature that is still able to sin. No longer will we have occasional forays into the land of self-indulgence. We will always say No as Jesus said No to all temptations. To silence the last lingering question that perhaps Jesus was sinless because He was God, the final generation will prove beyond a shadow of a doubt that men and women with fallen natures can live without sinning. This final demonstration will contribute to the vindication of God's character, His government, His justice, and His mercy—and the great controversy will be very near its conclusion.

Can we accept this challenge? "Christ took humanity and bore the hatred of the world that He might show men and women that they could *live without sin,* that their words, their actions, their spirit, might be sanctified to God. We can be *perfect Christians* if we will manifest this power in our lives."—*The Upward Look,* p. 303; emphasis supplied. God has promised that He can give victory over all sin. Because of this promise, biblical perfection should never be a discouraging topic; rather it should be the most glorious prospect ever set before God's people. God, in fact, is able to keep us from falling.